BEHIND THE GAS MASK

THOMAS I. FAITH

Behind the Gas Mask

THE U.S. CHEMICAL
WARFARE SERVICE
IN WAR AND PEACE

UNIVERSITY OF ILLINOIS PRESS
URBANA, CHICAGO, AND SPRINGFIELD

© 2014 by the Board of Trustees
of the University of Illinois
All rights reserved
Manufactured in the United States of America
1 2 3 4 5 C P 5 4 3 2 1

∞ This book is printed on acid-free paper.

Library of Congress Cataloging-in-Publication Data
Faith, Thomas I., 1979–
Behind the gas mask : the U.S. Chemical Warfare Service in war and peace / Thomas I. Faith.
pages cm
Includes bibliographical references and index.
ISBN 978-0-252-03868-6 (cloth : alk. paper) — ISBN 978-0-252-08026-5 (pbk. : alk. paper) — ISBN 978-0-252-09662-4 (e-book)
1. United States. Army. Chemical Warfare Service—History. 2. World War, 1914–1918—Chemical warfare. 3. World War, 1914–1918—United States. 4. Chemical warfare—United States—History—20th century. I. Title. II. Title: U.S. Chemical Warfare Service in war and peace.
UG447.F26   2014
358.'34097309041—dc23   2014005630

publication supported by
Figure Foundation
of peace and peace wings a future

Contents

Acknowledgments ix

Introduction 1

1 *Origins, 1917* 7
2 *Battle, 1918* 22
3 *Crisis, 1919–1920* 56
4 *Improvement, 1921–1925* 77
5 *Legacy, 1926–1929* 107

Notes 117
Bibliography 135
Index 145

Acknowledgments

This book was possible because of the resources I was privileged enough to be able to access, and I am grateful for all of the support I have been given over the last several years. I relied on the staff and collections at the National Archives at College Park, Maryland, and at the Library of Congress as I researched this manuscript. The Beckman Center for the History of Chemistry and the Othmer Library of Chemical History at the Chemical Heritage Foundation provided essential academic and financial support during the writing of this manuscript. I am grateful to the U.S. Army Center of Military History, the U.S. Army Heritage and Education Center, the Veterans History Project of the American Folklife Center, and the Smithsonian Libraries for making their collections available to me. I am also thankful for primary source materials made available online through the Google Books Library Project and the ProQuest Historical Newspapers database.

Special thanks to the Society for History in the Federal Government and the Council on America's Military Past for publishing articles based on the research for this manuscript while it was in progress. I would also like to thank the Society for Military History and the Beckman Center for the History of Chemistry for allowing me to present portions of this work. I sincerely appreciated the opportunities to receive feedback.

I am indebted to The George Washington University, the faculty, colleagues, and staff of the Department of History for their support through the research and writing of this manuscript. I would particularly like to thank Ronald Spector, Leo Ribuffo, Andrew Zimmerman, Joanna Spear, and Martin Sherwin. I am grateful to Joshua Botts for reviewing the manuscript's introduction and providing editorial guidance. I owe thanks also to the reviewers at the University of Illinois Press whose comments and criticisms helped me make substantial improvements and encouraged me to keep working.

I am grateful to my parents, Donald and Eileen, for all their love and support. I owe the most gratitude to my wife Julie, who is the greatest. I am dedicating this book to her.

BEHIND THE GAS MASK

Introduction

The first poison-gas attack experienced by the members of the 102nd Infantry Regiment occurred just before 7 P.M. on March 16, 1918, as they defended a one-kilometer portion of the Western Front extending from Mont des Tomes to the village of Pargny.[1] Many of these soldiers had heard about chemical weapon attacks from other U.S. Army units, as well as their British and French counterparts, and they remembered from training what to expect once the German gas artillery bombardment began. They discerned the distinctive odors of several types of gasses, including the pineapple aroma of tear gas, the musty lime smell of chlorine fumes, and the characteristic scent of mustard gas. The German attack employed a variety of chemical agents in an attempt to exploit any weaknesses in the soldiers' protective equipment or lapses in discipline.

Those who were able placed gas masks over their faces and adjusted the straps, nose clip, breathing hose, and filter box as they had been trained to do weeks before. Machine-gun crews threw protective blankets over their weapons to prevent contamination. Some soldiers, however, were confused or caught off guard. One entire company of front-line soldiers failed to realize they were being gassed until too late, and dozens of them suffered lung and eye injuries. A group of three signalmen and a runner put their gas masks on in time but pulled the top part of their facemasks down, exposing their eyes and noses to the poison gas, because they had difficulty seeing through the eye lenses. The German gas also contaminated some food rations, which had to be destroyed after the attack.

The gas shelling lasted until 9:50 P.M., ceased for several hours, then resumed again just before 1 A.M. to catch any soldiers who had taken their masks off to rest. The 102nd Infantry spent the night on alert, with their uncomfortable gas masks on, while fifteen thousand gas shells rained down on their position. After the attack the regiment's gas officer, Lt. Leonard J. Maloney, reported that "the men stood up splendidly under the heavy fire, and at no time was the morale weakened."[2] He noted, however, that at least eighty-five men were injured by the gas, and he characterized twelve of those injuries as "severe."[3] Like all the soldiers who were exposed to poison gas on the battlefields of World War I, every member of the 102nd Infantry, whether injured or not, would long remember the anxiety of this first experience with chemical warfare. As a weapon, poison gas spread apprehension even more effectively than it incapacitated enemy troops.

Americans and Europeans had recognized during the nineteenth century that poisonous gases could be weaponized, and in 1899 delegates at the Hague Convention outlawed the use of gas projectile weapons. The belligerent nations of the First World War were eager to develop new military technologies, however, and they marshaled chemists in order to wage chemical warfare. In 1915, Germany became the first belligerent nation to use lethal gas successfully, and other armies quickly followed. Although chemical warfare did not determine the outcome of World War I, the U.S. Army's struggle to adapt to this new method of war illuminated key dimensions of military planning and policy formation related to the adoption of new weapons technologies.

In 1921, Chief of the Chemical Warfare Service Amos A. Fries and fellow officer Clarence J. West defined five qualities that make a chemical usable as a weapon. First, they wrote, "it must be highly toxic" to serve its purpose.[4] The chemical must also "be readily manufactured in large quantities" to supply a vast military.[5] Although often described as gasses, chemical weapons needed to be stored and transported as pressurized liquids and be "more or less easily volatilized" to spread through the air once deployed.[6] Fries and West wrote furthermore that a chemical weapon "should have a considerably higher density than that of air" so that it would not rise and dissipate too quickly.[7] Finally, a chemical weapon needed to be chemically stable and relatively inert so that it would not change composition when it came into contact with other substances, such as its own metal storage container or rainwater. Meeting these requirements demanded specialists with expertise in many areas, including biology, chemistry, engineering, logistics, manufacturing, medicine, meteorology, and warcraft.

As this book will argue, the unique and multivariate requirements of chemical warfare posed serious challenges to existing U.S. military and scientific resources during the First World War. The inadequacy of preparedness efforts prior to U.S. entry into World War I in 1917 seriously hindered research, manufacturing, and training operations related to poison gas. At first, for expediency, specialists within existing organizations (including the Army Surgeon General's Office, the Ordnance Department, the Corps of Engineers, and a civilian federal agency called the Bureau of Mines) performed various chemical warfare responsibilities. These experts had difficulty coordinating their efforts and meeting their assigned duties with the time and resources they had available. Arriving in Europe in January 1918 with little training and no equipment, the officers of the Chemical Service Section (CSS) in the U.S. Corps of Engineers relied on the British and French armies for assistance. The British trained and equipped the CSS, which led the U.S. Army to organize its chemical warfare force similarly to the British Gas Service.[8] The CSS frequently coordinated its battlefield operations with the French Army and depended on them for logistical support.

In June 1918, CSS officers successfully consolidated their authority over the U.S. chemical warfare program under the auspices of a new Chemical Warfare Service (CWS). Unfortunately, this administrative change did not guarantee tangible improvements in the military's ability to defend soldiers from poison gas, its capacity to employ chemical weapons in battle, or its capability to manufacture chemical warfare equipment during the remaining months of the war. The American Expeditionary Force (AEF) remained inadequately trained and ill equipped to defend itself against poison-gas attacks. The United States suffered a higher percentage of gas casualties than any other nation during World War I, and chemical weapons earned a reputation for being cruel and barbaric among soldiers and civilians alike.

The CWS's transition to a peacetime military organization after World War I represents a critical turning point in the history of chemical warfare, when U.S. chemical warriors had to confront widespread negative views about chemical weapons in the United States to defend their mission and adequately prepare the country for a future chemical war. As the military shrank to accommodate its diminished budget after the 1918 armistice, Congress and the Department of War targeted the chemical weapons program for elimination. Civilian peace activists lobbied against chemical weapons as manifestations of the evils of war, and the Department of State pursued international agreements to prevent chemical warfare in future conflicts. CWS officers fundamentally disagreed with those who characterized chemical weapons as barbaric. For these chemical warfare experts, poison gas represented an advanced tool of national defense, and they considered its detractors misinformed.

Earl J. Atkisson, the commander of the U.S. chemical warfare regiment in France during World War I, believed that opposition to chemical weapons reflected a "natural but sentimental tendency of people to attach all the terrible aspects of war to its latest phases of development." Atkisson wrote that "war is abhorrent to the individual, yet he accepts blowing men to pieces with high explosive, mowing men down with machine guns, and even sinking a battleship in mid-ocean with its thousand or fifteen hundred men being carried to certain death. He has grown accustomed to these things and tacitly admits their necessity. However, to burn the skin of a man outrages all his civilized instincts."[9]

Modern-day scholars still disagree about the extent to which chemical weapons deserve to be regarded as a separate, more terrible class of weapons. The fact that average individuals remain convinced that chemical weapons belong in a discrete category indicates that there is something about those weapons that people consider unacceptable. But there is some truth to the arguments made by Atkisson and others that chemical weapons are not any worse than other weapons in terms of their destructive power. While the current study does evaluate many of the arguments made by members of the CWS, I attempted to remain objective with respect to the morality of chemical warfare. The ethical implications of chemical weapons defy objective empirical analysis, and opinions about them are generally formed by one's personal values.

Amos A. Fries, the chief of the CWS, wrote that, during the postwar years, his organization "had to fight for its very existence."[10] Fries led his fellow officers in an extensive public relations campaign to promote chemical warfare as the "newest and cheapest, the most mysterious, the least understood, the most powerful, and the least appreciated method of warfare known to man."[11] The gas warfare soldiers worked with partners in the U.S. chemical industry and with sympathetic members of Congress to ensure that the CWS remained an independent service within the army under the National Defense Act of 1920. Afterward, the CWS continued its public relations campaign to convince other members of the military and the American public that chemical weapons were more advanced and humane than projectile weapons and that poison-gas research had peacetime uses, such as the development of insecticides and law enforcement tools. By working in concert with allies in the chemical industry and Congress, members of the CWS were able to change threatening military policies while collaterally influencing a variety of public policies, including veterans' compensation, tariffs on dyes and other chemicals, and capital punishment. The CWS in the 1920s showed how a motivated group successfully affected national public policy.

Like all public relations campaigns, however, the CWS's advertisements did not always reflect reality, and its methods were not always commendable. CWS officers falsely claimed that exposure to poison gas could cure respiratory ailments and insinuated that pacifist and women's organizations were communist bulwarks. Fries hoped that gas troops would one day fight as part of every army and division in the military, predicting, "Chemical Warfare will endure in the future, despite all opposition."[12] But while the CWS's accomplishments during the First World War and the postwar period were significant, the organization and its allies in the domestic chemical industry and Congress failed to mobilize public opinion to support the use of chemical weapons in future wars. The American people remained skeptical that poison gasses were humane weapons, and U.S. foreign policymakers worked to ensure that they would not be used in future conflicts. In the 1920s, U.S. negotiators secured international agreements that outlawed the use of chemical weapons. It took time for the United States and other nations to ratify formal international prohibitions of chemical weapons but, in the interim, strong international norms against their use mostly prevented their employment. The story of the CWS suggests that the autonomy of the national defense partnership known as the military-industrial complex can be limited when policymakers confront pervasive, hostile public opinion.

This book is an institutional history of the U.S. Army organization responsible for chemical warfare, from its creation through Fries's departure from the service in 1929. It explores how and why chemical warfare work continued in the United States after the armistice ended World War I. Chapter 1 describes the chemical warfare program as it rapidly developed in the United States before the nation began sending soldiers to fight in France. Chapter 2 describes the AEF's experiences with poison gas on the Western Front and the logistical effort made by the United States to support chemical warfare. Chapter 3 relates the CWS's struggle to continue chemical weapons work in a hostile political environment as the U.S. Army sought to digest the lessons learned from the Great War under the budget constraints of the postwar period. Chapter 4 highlights the CWS's efforts to improve its public image and its reputation in the military in the first half of the 1920s. Finally, chapter 5 discusses the successes and failures of the CWS during the second half of the 1920s, in light of the organization's ultimate incapacity to influence foreign policy. Although the United States has demurred at using chemical weapons since World War I, it maintained chemical warfare capability through the end of the Cold War. Ultimately, the history of the CWS illuminates the relationship between innovation, memory, institutional development, and national policy.

1 Origins, 1917

Despite ample warning that U.S. soldiers would need to be prepared to face poison gas, preparations for chemical warfare waited till almost the last minute. Once the Department of War began making arrangements to enlist, train, and equip the American Expeditionary Force (AEF) to join a war that in 1917 was already in full swing, the nation's political and military leaders hoped that the doughboys would soon be ready to fight on equal footing with the British, the French, and the rest of their allies. Nevertheless, the U.S. Army's lack of prior experience with gas and its dearth of chemical warfare equipment guaranteed that it would depend on British and French assistance during World War I. The United States spent 1917 rapidly and haphazardly cobbling together a chemical warfare organization that needed to be capable of a variety of responsibilities that included performing research, manufacturing war gasses and gas masks, training the soldiers of the AEF to defend themselves against enemy gas, and also deploying gas on the battlefield. The members of the U.S. chemical warfare program performed well under the circumstances, but more advanced preparation would have improved readiness and mitigated the need for emergency measures.

The first proposals to use gas as a weapon in the United States were made during the Civil War. A schoolteacher in New York named John W. Doughty wrote to the White House in 1862 to suggest that cannon shells filled with chlorine gas be used against the Confederates. A member of President Abraham Lincoln's staff forwarded the letter to the Department of War, where the idea was not pursued.[1] In 1864 Forest Shepherd, a professor at Western Reserve University, proposed a formula for a noxious gas cloud that he hoped the Army of the Potomac could use to break the stalemate at the siege of Petersburg. That suggestion was refused by the commanding general, Ulysses S. Grant. A host of other proposals to use various nonlethal chemicals also circulated on both the Union and Confederate sides, but ultimately the U.S. Civil War avoided becoming the first chemical war in modern world history.[2]

With growing concern about the destructive capabilities of nineteenth-century weapons, the Russian Empire hosted a conference of European delegates to discuss the laws of war in 1868. The declaration they produced in St. Petersburg did not address chemical weapons specifically, but it did document their resolve to fix "the technical limits at which the necessities of war ought to yield to the requirements of humanity," and to renounce "the employment of arms which uselessly aggravate the sufferings of disabled men, or render their death inevitable."[3] The St. Petersburg Declaration only expressly outlawed exploding bullets, but the contracting parties acknowledged the possibility that future scientific advancements in weaponry would merit additional arms limitation agreements "to conciliate the necessities of war with the laws of humanity."[4] Attendees at successive Hague Peace Conferences in 1899 and 1907 used the language of the St. Petersburg Declaration to guide their discussions of the various arms-limitation conventions they considered. Deciding that the use of poison-gas weapons would be inhumane, the Hague Peace Conference of 1899 issued a declaration that required the contracting nations "to abstain from the use of projectiles the object of which is the diffusion of asphyxiating or deleterious gasses."[5] In spite of the fact that this Hague Declaration was in force during the First World War among all of the belligerent nations, the agreement did not prevent poison gas from being used.

World War I broke out in August 1914, and it defied predictions that the fighting would be over quickly. The German army overran most of Belgium and advanced rapidly into northern France before it was stopped at the Marne River in September. Afterward the French and the Germans raced their armies north while trying to outflank each other, extending their lines to the English Channel. The British army arrived in time to join the French and Belgians at Ypres, where the Germans were stopped again and the front stabilized for the winter. Both the Germans and the Allied powers dug in and prepared for the war on Germany's "Western Front" to last through the spring.

Even before the stalemate occurred, the French army used tear gas in battle against the Germans—gas grenades that had originally been developed for riot control, but in such small concentrations that their

German opponents failed to notice. German chemists, however, were already proposing that their nation's vast chemical resources be marshaled to the cause. The German chemical industry was ready to produce many kinds of war gasses, and the army was willing to employ new weapons that could give its soldiers a battlefield advantage. The military may also have suspected that the French and British were designing similar weapons. Chemistry professor and future Nobel laureate Walther Nernst designed an artillery shell filled with a chemical irritant that was used against the British near Neuve-Chapelle in October 1914. Three thousand of these shells were fired during the battle, but the substance failed to have any effect. In January the Germans launched an assault against the Russians on the eastern front in Poland, at Bolimov, using eighteen thousand tear gas "T-shells." The winter temperature prevented the xylyl bromide in the T-shells from vaporizing, however, and the gas was completely ineffective.[6]

Despite how poorly chemical munitions had performed thus far, Germany continued to develop the technology. Fritz Haber, another future Nobel laureate in chemistry, advocated the use of lethal and widely available chlorine gas, and he devised an alternative method of delivering it. Instead of using shells or grenades, which could only spread small quantities of gas and technically violated the 1899 Hague Declaration against asphyxiating gas projectiles, Haber suggested that the chlorine be released from storage cylinders and allowed to drift across to the enemy trenches with the prevailing wind. Under Haber's supervision the soldiers of Pioneer Regiment 35 spent weeks preparing the first cylinder attack near Ypres. They moved thousands of chlorine cylinders into position and then waited for the wind to blow the right direction and speed. At dusk on April 22, 1915, the Pioneers connected the cylinders to long hoses that led out in front of their trench and opened the valves to release the poisonous gas into the air. The breeze carried the chlorine west along the ground to the unsuspecting soldiers in its path.[7]

The Ypres attack was devastating for the British, Canadian, French, and Algerian soldiers who were caught in the gas cloud. Without protective masks of any kind, the choking soldiers dropped their weapons and equipment and ran from the front lines trying to escape the poison air. "Some got away in time," according to a British news cable to the *New York Times*, "but many, alas, not understanding the new danger, were not so fortunate and were overcome by the fumes and died poisoned. Among those who escaped, nearly all cough and spit blood, the chlorine attacking the mucous membrane. The dead were turned black at once."[8] For the German army, the attack seemed extraordinarily successful. The

Germans who followed the deadly cloud into their enemy's trenches encountered little or no resistance from soldiers or artillery. The French and British were able to mount a hurried defense, but they suffered a loss of territory and an estimated five thousand casualties in the gas attack.[9]

In the aftermath, Germany was vilified by the international press and by foreign leaders. The commander of British forces in World War I, Sir John French, said that he regretted "the fighting has been characterized on the enemy's side, by cynical and barbarous disregard of the well-known usages of civilized war and by flagrant disregard of the Hague convention."[10] For many observers, Germany's use of chemical weapons, combined with the invasion of neutral Belgium at the start of the war and the May 1915 sinking of the passenger ship RMS *Lusitania*, seemed all to support claims that Germany was an especially barbarous and bloodthirsty nation. The *New York Times* reported that the German nation and people were being denounced in the Russian press with such statements as "the Germans have turned this war into warfare against humanity at large. They are not content with killing their foes, but must murder every living thing they have a chance to destroy."[11] Even as they denounced the German army as barbarous, the British and French raced to create their own lethal chemical weapons to use in retaliation.[12]

On September 24, 1915, the British launched their first large chlorine cylinder attack against the Germans near Loos, Belgium. They released 150 tons of the gas and, in spite of the calm weather, hoped the breeze would be strong enough to carry the poison cloud across the field as it had for the Germans at Ypres. The gas moved too slowly in the sluggish wind, and while some of the chlorine reached the German lines, some of it settled around the British soldiers in their trenches instead. The incident vividly demonstrated the problem with relying on prevailing weather conditions to deliver chemical weapons, but overall the Allies remained convinced that poison gas was effective, and they resolved to continue its use.[13]

As the war on the Western Front continued through 1915, the British, French, and Germans continued to develop more potent poisonous gasses, more reliable delivery systems, and more effective defensive measures. By the end of the year, all of the combatants had managed to design and manufacture gas masks that could protect their soldiers from chlorine gas. Accordingly, they began to research and develop new types of poison gasses to use against each other. On December 19, 1915, Germany introduced phosgene on the battlefield, gassing the British at Ypres. Phosgene is a more lethal agent than chlorine, and it could not be filtered out of the air by conventional gas masks. Fortunately for the British, their military had realized months earlier that phosgene could potentially be used as a weapon, and the soldiers at Ypres had been issued masks that could defend against it. Despite the existence of these improved gas filters, the British and French began to manufacture and use the new gas as well, and phosgene ultimately caused more casualties than any other gas during World War I.[14] In May 1916 the Germans released yet another new war gas, diphosgene, which rendered masks designed to protect against phosgene obsolete, necessitating a new round of improvements.[15]

Because gas masks could allow soldiers to survive a chemical attack unharmed, poison gas had to be deployed creatively in order to be an effective weapon. Chemical attacks could be timed to surprise the enemy and catch soldiers who failed to put their masks on quickly enough. Other gas attacks were designed to keep poison in the air persistently, long enough to outlast the enemy's gas-mask filters, forcing them either to evacuate the area or to change masks and risk breathing the chemicals. The armies on the Western Front also experimented with different chemical combinations during attacks. Simultaneous use of nonlethal irritants or tear gasses could force suffering soldiers to take their masks off, thereby exposing them to lethal asphyxiants. Alternating the use of visible smoke clouds and an invisible gas, like chlorine, could give enemy soldiers the impression that a poison-gas attack was longer lasting and more severe than it actually was. Using poison gas in concert with a barrage of shrapnel-filled artillery shells could cause injuries, confusion, and destruction as defenders struggled to don their masks. When a soldier was able to get his mask on in time and stay safe, gas would nevertheless remain a powerful threat to morale. Wearing an uncomfortable mask, unable to doze, breathing through a hose and a charcoal filter with poison air swirling around him could make a soldier miserable and terrified.[16]

In view of the fact that launching gas from cylinders could expose your own soldiers to the poison, and because the method depended on favorable weather conditions, all the armies of the Western Front experimented with safer and more reliable methods of deploying chemical weapons on the battlefield in 1915 and 1916. Gas-filled artillery shells were developed that could be filled with adequate amounts of chemicals, fly on trajectory, and disperse the contents effectively on detonation. The warring nations also used mortars to fire small, gas-filled canisters at enemy troops. As new chemical warfare devices were perfected, the use of cylinders to spread poison gas became less common. British Director of Gas Services Charles H. Foulkes continued to favor cylinders over other gas-delivery systems but was virtually alone in that regard.[17]

In 1916 the British introduced a chemical warfare device called a Livens projector. It was a large metal tube, open at one end, which was installed by partially burying it in the ground at an angle. The open end pointed up at the target and a large metal drum full of poisonous gas was lowered inside. Livens projectors were usually installed together in groups of hundreds and were launched electrically from a remote location. When triggered, the projectors would send the hundreds of gas-filled drums sailing through the air toward enemy targets, where they would explode and disperse a dense cloud of poisonous vapors. Installing Livens projectors was labor-intensive work that took days or weeks, and each one could only be used for a single launch, but the devices had substantial advantages. With little or no warning, projectors blanketed a target in a large amount of poison gas, and, because the drums were were launched remotely, enemy retaliatory fire would cause no casualties. Called by one historian "the most-feared chemical weapon of the war," Livens projectors were a salient feature of combat on the Western Front by 1917.[18]

Given that these conditions existed during the First World War in Europe, the failure of the United States to prepare for chemical warfare is perplexing. One reason Americans may have been slow to organize chemical warfare activities was the unchivalrous stereotype that poison gas had. Some members of the military saw gas as a weapon that did not befit a soldier, and they may have dragged their feet preparing to use it against an enemy.[19] Another reason related to the fact that all news about the Western Front arrived in the United States through European censors. Assistant Secretary of War and Director of Munitions Benedict Crowell wrote with hindsight that "during the spring and summer of 1917 two marked tendencies were to be observed in the fighting in France. One of these was the greatly increased use by both sides of poisonous gases and chemicals, frightful in their effect; the other the almost complete censorship that hid the knowledge of this tendency not only from the people of Europe but particularly from those of the newest belligerent, America."[20]

British and French propagandists trumpeted news of the first German poison-gas attack at Ypres as evidence of the enemy's barbarity, but subsequent gas attacks received less or no publicity.[21] Crowell speculated that "the British and French Governments, who then controlled all news from the front, feared, and perhaps with reason, that if the picture of gas warfare, as it was then developing, should be placed before the American people, it would result in an unreasonable dread of gasses on the part of the American Nation and its soldiers."[22] Britain and France feared that too much information about chemical combat would make American participation in the war less likely, but the "news blackout" had the unintended consequence of hindering preparedness. After Congress declared war against Germany on April 6, 1917, European allies seem to have freely shared military and scientific information about poison gas and provided material support.[23] Documents, equipment, and even personnel were made available to the United States over the course of World War I, but allied assistance could not help the American army compensate for systemic inexperience.

Whatever the reason, the U.S. military displayed a clear pattern of inactivity before 1917 with regard to poison gas. There appears to have been no attempt to prepare for chemical weapons on the battlefield before November 1916, when Secretary of War Newton D. Baker assigned Army Surgeon General William C. Gorgas responsibility for designing and developing gas masks. Under Gorgas, the Medical Department began some preliminary research but allowed the project to languish before a mask could be designed.[24] By February 1917, two months before the U.S. declaration of war, neither a single gas mask nor any other piece of chemical warfare equipment had been manufactured for the army. That month the Department of War lost the initiative to a civilian agency within the Department of the Interior.

Recognizing that war with Germany and its allies was a possibility, Secretary of the Interior Franklin K. Lane asked every bureau and agency under his authority to come up with ways they could potentially assist the nation in the event that war was declared. An office called the Bureau of Mines volunteered to be the government agency responsible for chemical warfare. The Bureau of Mines dealt with mine safety, commodities, and environmental effects, and it had experience with the poisonous gasses that created hazardous conditions for miners underground. The bureau was already equipped with research facilities, experienced technical and scientific personnel, and it had professional relationships with related civilian manufacturing industries.[25] While mineshaft gasses and manmade chemical weapons are very different, the Bureau of Mines seemed to be a fitting place for chemical weapons work to begin.

As soon as the director of the Bureau of Mines, Van H. Manning, received approval from the Secretary of the Interior, Manning approached the Department of War with the offer of assistance. Representatives from the Department of War met with the Bureau of Mines at the U.S. Army War College in Carlisle, Pennsylvania, "enthusiastically" accepted Manning's offer, and promised support.[26] Manning delegated all Bureau of Mines chemical warfare activities to a branch called the Gas Investigations Division, under the leadership of George A. Burrell, and the two men began working with deliberate speed. Manning and Burrell reached out to a network of other related agencies and organizations outside the Department of the Interior and used the resources of the National Research Council to begin chemical warfare research as quickly and efficiently as possible. They created a partnership with the U.S. Army Medical Department to resuscitate military gas-mask research. They also sought out assistance from major universities, scientific organizations, and research agencies throughout the United States.[27]

In July 1917, with war now officially declared, American University in Washington, D.C., offered the Bureau of Mines two of its buildings, rent free, for use as research facilities for the duration of the war. The university asked only that some laboratory improvements that the bureau planned to make to the existing buildings become the school's permanent property once the war ended. The bureau accepted the offer, completed the new construction, and began moving personnel there on September 15, 1917. The American University research station became their main facility, but the Bureau of Mines also established research laboratories under similar arrangements at other institutions, such as Catholic University, Johns Hopkins, Harvard, Princeton, Yale, Ohio State, Rice Institute, MIT, Worcester Polytechnic, and the National Carbon Company and General Electric's National Electric Light Association laboratory (both in Cleveland, Ohio).[28]

"The outstanding feature of the entire program undertaken by this industrial army," a history produced by General Electric declared, "was the quickness with which large organizations, efficiently handled, were able to adapt their immense resources and trained personnel to the war needs of the government."[29] The Bureau of Mines had been able to build a national network of organizations to facilitate chemical warfare research in a matter of months. Until the Department of War began to contribute funds in July 1917, the Bureau of Mines funded 100 percent of the cost of this work.[30] The number of university-trained chemists at work on war gasses was a factor that separated the United States from other nations fighting the First World War. A far higher percentage of unqualified personnel or technical-college graduates were behind the poison-gas programs in Britain and Germany.[31]

Manning was able to recruit chemists from a variety of public and private institutions for work in the Gas Investigations Division of the Bureau of Mines. The country's chemists were eager to use their training and skills to serve their nation in its hour of need, and they seemed to have no reservations about working on chemical weapons. One of the first people Manning hired was Bradley Dewey, the research chemist at the American Tin Plate Company in Pittsburgh. Another scientist recruited at the outset was Warren K. Lewis, assistant professor of chemical engineering at MIT. Both of them were sought out not only for their technical experience but also for their energy and enthusiasm for the work, characteristics the Bureau of Mines sought in every chemist recruited for gas research.[32]

Chief chemist for the Bureau of Mines, Charles L. Parsons, wrote of World War I gas research that "one of the most interesting features of this work was the sprit shown by American chemists and the immediate response made by practically every chemist in America to the call to duty. The organization was rapidly built up and contained the names of the most prominent chemists in the country, as well as those of hundreds of young chemists who would later become prominent."[33] Parsons himself was later recognized as one of the most distinguished scientists in the United States, receiving the American Chemical Society's Priestly Medal in 1932.[34] When the U.S. Army established the combat arm of the chemical warfare effort in December 1917, the bureau transferred many of its trained personnel to the new unit for service in France. The bulk of the men who first served in what would later be called the Chemical Warfare Service were recruited and trained by the Bureau of Mines.[35]

While these chemists all worked on chemical warfare research projects under the general direction of Manning and Burrell, they performed the work at their branch laboratories across the country. According to the General Electric Company, "the policy the Bureau of Mines had originally adopted was to start investigations independently at a number of places. The most successful process evolved, either through the individual or combined efforts of the different organizations working on the problem, was to be adopted by the government."[36] This was a highly unusual dynamic for many businesses, one that sometimes resulted in "two rival organizations working harmoniously together on the same problem."[37] Cooperation was essential, since scientific research is a process that is generally measured in years, not months or weeks. The urgent need for chemical warfare equipment, particularly gas masks, made speed critical.[38]

The Bureau of Mines conducted experiments and wrote reports on practically every aspect of gas-mask development through summer 1917. Much of their experimentation tested different substances in gas-mask filters, in an attempt to find the most chemically absorbent material that would provide wearers with the best protection. That was a more difficult task than perhaps it sounds, because the mask filter had to block a variety of different poisonous gasses soldiers were likely to encounter, while still allowing soldiers to breathe. Industry experts recognized that most people believed "'charcoal is charcoal,' just as 'pigs is pigs,' but, as a matter of fact, there are as many different kinds of charcoal as there are woods from which the charcoal is derived. And there are also many varied methods of preparing charcoal from any particular wood."[39] Bureau of Mines researchers were able to quickly determine that charcoal made from burnt coconut shell, due to its high density, made the best filter of all the commercially available alternatives. Throughout their participation in the war, the bureau continued the work to refine methods of producing charcoal in sufficient quantities and configurations for use in American gas masks.[40]

Face pieces for the masks were primarily designed by rubber companies around Akron, Ohio. The Goodrich Company, Goodyear Tire & Rubber, and the United States Rubber Company, although competitors in their industry, collaborated to design flexible, rubber-coated materials that would fit tightly around the face so as not allow poison gas to penetrate.[41] The shape of the mask had to be such that the mask would fit a variety of different face contours and head sizes without letting air in around the edges. At the same time, a mask that fit too tightly around the forehead, jaw, or throat could cause headaches and choking.[42]

Of course, allies such as Britain and France had already developed their own gas masks, and information about their manufacture was available to scientists in the United States. One could question the logic of engineering a new mask design when it would have been simpler for the AEF to rely on an existing one. Protective masks, though, were still relatively new battlefield innovations. While researchers in the United States were able to study gas masks manufactured by all the belligerent nations, they were also able to identify aspects of each that could be improved. National pride may also have been a factor, since all of the First World War participants had designed masks of their own.

But the U.S. soldiers preparing to fight in France would need gas masks sooner than the Bureau of Mines could produce them. While research was proceeding quickly, there was not enough time to accomplish the work required. On May 16, 1917, Acting Chief of Staff Tasker H. Bliss ordered the surgeon general to begin manufacturing poison-gas defensive equipment, including twenty-five thousand gas masks that were needed immediately for the first group of U.S. soldiers training to go overseas.[43] Major L. P. Williamson of the Army Medical Department coordinated with Manning at the Bureau of Mines to get production started. To expedite the process, the bureau obtained gas masks used by the British, called Small Box Respirators (SBRs), and worked to copy them. Manning asked Bradley Dewey to coordinate the manufacturing effort.[44] Crowell's description of where the various elements of the masks were fabricated illustrates the great difficulty of Dewey's task:

The production of these first 25,000 masks called upon the services of various manufacturers. The assembling of the masks was conducted by the American Can Co., at Brooklyn, N. Y. The B. F. Goodrich Co., of Akron, manufactured the face pieces with the eyepieces inserted, also the connecting hose, the check valve of the canister, the flutter valve, and the rubber mouthpiece. The American Can Co. produced the canisters. The Day Chemical Co., of Westline, Pa., gave the charcoal its first burning. The Ward Baking Co., of Brooklyn, patriotically baked the charcoal—to activate it—in their bread ovens free of charge. The General Chemical Co., of New York, supplied the soda-lime granules. The Doehler Die Casting Co., of Brooklyn, manufactured the angle tubes. The Simmons Hardware Co., of St. Louis, produced the waterproof knapsacks. The Seaver Howland Press, of Boston, printed the cards of instructions that went with the mask outfit; and the Beetle & MacLean Manufacturing Co., of Boston, printed the record tags.[45]

In less than one month, 20,088 of the SBR copies were mass-produced and shipped to England for inspection, with the remaining five thousand soon to follow.[46] Prudently, the Bureau of Mines and the Medical Department asked British experts to test the masks before they were issued to U.S. soldiers. The British found all of the masks defective and unsuitable for use. They determined that the face piece was vulnerable to a particular type of war gas, chloropicrin, and the soda-lime granules in the filter tended to clump and block the passage of breathable air.[47] After this failed effort, the Department of War decided it would need to purchase and issue foreign masks from the British and French while chemists in the United States worked to improve their design.

Gas-mask research received priority from the Bureau of Mines, but an important battlefield development in July 1917 forced them to expand into the field of offensive-gas research. On July 12 the Germans used a new type of chemical weapon against British defenders at Ypres. First termed HS (Hun Stuff) or Yperite, the yellowish, garlic-smelling liquid came to be called mustard gas. The soldiers who were exposed to mustard gas found it caused no symptoms in the first few hours. After that, however, victims experienced severe conjunctivitis, stomach pains, and vomiting. Whereas the war gasses that had been used in World War I prior to this had primarily affected the victim's lungs, mustard gas caused chemical burns. A patient's skin would appear severely irritated at first before vesicles and large blisters formed over the exposed areas. Their mouth, nose, throat, and lungs could also be burned by the chemical, making it difficult, and perhaps impossible, for those exposed to breathe.[48]

Doctors found that some mustard-gas patients would recover within weeks on a regimen of rest and care, while others could sustain permanent injury to the eyes and lungs, and some died from the gas outright or from subsequent respiratory infections. The burns and inflammation were found to develop even with exposure to very low concentrations of the gas, and the effects of the gas seemed to worsen with increased atmospheric humidity. Mustard gas also had a very high persistency that left gassed areas, clothing, and equipment hazardous for days and even weeks after exposure.[49] The future chief of the Chemical Warfare Service, Amos A. Fries, wrote of mustard gas, "It is the king of all gasses. It changed not alone gas warfare, but to a considerable extent all warfare."[50]

The king of gasses posed a grave new challenge to the allies fighting Germany, but it presented U.S. scientists with an opportunity to be active participants in a critical new research effort wherein their inexperience with other war gasses would not necessarily be a disadvantage. It only took days for British chemists to identify the chemical formula for mustard gas from samples taken after the Ypres attack, and they shared that information with the Bureau of Mines and the Department of War.[51] Afterward, experts working on mustard gas in Britain, France, and the United States continued to share results with one another, but they conducted their own separate research projects within their independent organizations. This working arrangement resulted in a duplication of effort.

The Bureau of Mines and the U.S. Army Medical Department studied the pathology of mustard gas (along with that of the other, older war gasses) through experiments on animals. Fries once described these experiments to a Senate subcommittee, saying, "We take the best possible care of all those animals so that they get the least possible suffering."[52]

> What we do in chemical warfare, when we get a new substance, is to take a small quantity and start in trying it out on white mice. Now, we have a regular scale known as the toxicity or poisonous scale of several hundreds of chemicals, and they are all referred to white mice. Some of them have been extended finally to some of the larger animals. If we find that substance of considerable danger to these white mice we deduce at once that it will be relatively dangerous to the human being, and right away we can begin to undertake such preparations as we can think of to protect men working with that substance, or who may meet it anywhere.[53]

Researchers at the Bureau of Mines and the U.S. Army Medical Department attempted numerous treatments for gas poisoning, including blood transfusions and sanitary regimens. They also tried to develop burn ointments and salves to help alleviate the pain and itching. One group of experiments recommended cleaning mustard-gas victims with kerosene or acetone to wash off the poison, in what was clearly not a pleasant or especially safe therapy. None of these experiments led to promising treatments. The medical scientists who advised the Bureau of Mines concluded that "the treatment of a fully developed 'mustard' burn is at best very unsatisfactory. Little more can be done than attempt to keep the lesion sterile throughout the course of its very sluggish healing. Emphasis should therefore be placed particularly upon prevention of the burn rather than upon treatment."[54]

Chemists in the United States had more success developing the manufacturing process used to make mustard gas. When British experts first identified the substance as mustard gas, after it was used on their army at Ypres, the only known method of synthesizing it (described by a German chemist, Victor Meyer, in the nineteenth century) was a time-consuming process that yielded only small quantities.[55] Chemists in Britain and the United States worked independently to develop a method of mass-producing the large quantities of mustard that would be needed for use against the enemy. Sir William Pope at Cambridge University led the British research effort, and Harvard chemist James B. Conant directed the work at the American University research station in the United States. Pope and Conant discovered the same mass-production method nearly simultaneously in January 1918, though Pope earned the credit by announcing his results first.[56]

In addition to protective masks and mustard gas, the Bureau of Mines also experimented with lower-priority chemical substances related to the war. They conducted extensive tests that were designed to find a substitute for hydrogen in zeppelins, ultimately identifying helium as the most promising alternative. They also tested various incendiary chemicals to find the best smoke-producing agents for smoke screens, which were designed to shield troop and ship movement from enemy observation.[57]

While heady progress was being made in chemical research at the Bureau of Mines during the months that followed the declaration of war, there was growing concern within the Department of War that other gas preparations were falling behind in the summer of 1917. The twenty-five thousand gas masks that had been ordered from the Surgeon General's Office were defective, and no training program was yet in place to prepare U.S. soldiers for chemical weapons on the battlefield. In July the Department of War reworked chemical warfare responsibilities in a way they hoped would speed up preparations.[58] Under the new organizational arrangement, the Bureau of Mines remained at the center of the national chemical warfare establishment, performing research and development;

but other responsibilities, and some of their personnel, were parsed off to a variety of military agencies. Responsibility for manufacturing defensive chemical warfare tools, like gas masks, remained with the U.S. Army Surgeon General's Office, which, as a medical arm of the military, was considered the best agency to protect soldiers from the physical effects of chemical weapons. Offensive chemical-warfare tools, such as artillery shells, were entrusted to the U.S. Army Ordnance Department, which supplied the military with weapons and was viewed as the best choice for chemical weapons procurement. The Army Corps of Engineers, finally, was responsible for the battlefield use of all this equipment. Their personnel had the technical expertise needed. The Bureau of Mines promised to coordinate all of its research activities with these various organizations and to work according to their specifications.[59]

Also in July the acting chief of staff for the U.S. Army ordered the Surgeon General's Office to provide nine gas-defense instructors for a military training school in Oklahoma. Needless to say, none of the medical officers who could potentially serve as gas instructors in compliance with the order had any experience with gas warfare.[60] The Surgeon General's Office did not provide the instructors until the end of August, and once gas-defensive training began in earnest in September, the effort was plagued with difficulties. Shortages of equipment and instructional materials, and the lack of expert instructors rendered the training program insufficient. As the first wave of U.S. soldiers prepared to sail to France that fall, the Department of War approached Britain with hat in hand. Allied Britain was asked to send gas-warfare instructors to America to train soldiers before they could embark for Europe. Britain not only sent dozens of instructors who arrived in October, but their commanding officer, Samuel J. M. Auld, agreed to write a gas-warfare manual for the U.S. Army to use as its primary instructional text. The army also took the responsibility for gas-defense training from the Surgeon General's Office and vested it with the Army Corps of Engineers, at Auld's suggestion.[61]

While training operations were underway, the Ordnance Department began chemical-weapons manufacturing operations. They found some private manufacturers who were willing, and able, to produce poison gas and related equipment, but in most cases chemical weapons had to be manufactured by the military. Chemical weapons and their delivery systems had never been manufactured in the United States before on a scale that the army would require, so the necessary machinery and personnel were in short supply. There were also no known peacetime uses for chemical weapons, so whatever changes were made to a factory during the war would be of no use after the fighting. Furthermore, civilians were extremely reluctant to perform chemical-weapons work because of the inherent danger.

The Ordnance Department was also not able to find any private firms willing to perform shell filling in 1917. Once artillery shells and poison gas had been manufactured at their respective factories, a third location was required to fill the shells with the gas. According to Chemical Warfare Service officers, no manufacturer was willing to operate a poison-gas shell-filling plant because they "recognized that the manufacture of such material would be attended by a very great danger; that the work would be limited to the duration of the war; and the processes involved, as well as the plants necessary for carrying out their processes, would have little post-war value."[62] The U.S. Army Ordnance Department therefore resolved to construct a shell-filling plant of its own in the summer of 1917.

The site selected for the new plant was a thirty-five-thousand-acre piece of land near Aberdeen, Maryland, along the Pennsylvania Railroad near the Chesapeake Bay; construction began there on November 15. Originally called Gunpowder Reservation, the name was later changed to Edgewood Arsenal. The shell-filling plant was described as "really composed of several small plants, each of which was made up of units radiating from a central refrigeration plant which would serve all the units. Each unit could then be fitted with machinery adapted for filling shells of a different size and for a particular gas. Moreover, an accident in one of the units would in no way impair the working of the remainder."[63] The interior of each plant was as automated as the technology of the period would allow and was designed to keep the workers as safe as possible, with the shell-filling operation "carried out in a thoroughly ventilated room or tunnel, arranged so that the machinery in the tunnel could be operated from the outside."[64]

The shell-filling plant was still in the process of being completed at the end of 1917; however, the Ordnance Department was already making plans to expand. Bids were being collected from contractors to build several chemical factories at Edgewood Arsenal, but no useable gas masks or chemical weapons had yet been produced. Despite what U.S. chemical-weapons workers had been able to accomplish over the previous year, the first American soldiers arriving in France in 1918 would have to rely on British and French gas-warfare equipment.

2 Battle, 1918

The chemical warfare organization that had evolved in the United States in 1917 had to support battlefield operations in 1918. The American Expeditionary Force (AEF) began to arrive in Europe, where it faced poison gas. On the whole, the nascent Chemical Warfare Service found itself seriously challenged by conditions on the Western Front and dependent on U.S. allies for information and equipment. The gas-mask training that soldiers of the AEF were given proved to be inadequate, and they suffered comparatively heavy gas casualties in the fighting. The AEF favored the use of more conventional weapons and therefore made only limited use of chemical weapons against the Germans. The U.S. Army's inability to organize for chemical warfare in the time they had available delegitimized the gas warfare program and jeopardized the program's status after World War I ended.

All U.S. soldiers preparing to serve in France in 1918 needed to know what to do in the event of a gas attack, and it was because of the importance and urgency of this task that the training responsibilities of the Surgeon General's Office were reassigned to the Corps of Engineers in late 1917. The Corps of Engineers established the Chemical Service Section (CSS), also known simply as the Gas Service, and staffed it with chemists and engineers who were expected to bring speed and expertise to the assignment. The officers who conducted the training nevertheless lacked resources and support. They attempted to set up chemical warfare training facilities at the cantonments where the AEF was assembling across the United States, but they were plagued by shortages of equipment and lacked up-to-date instructional manuals. Moreover, the officers of the

CSS themselves had only limited experience with chemical weapons. In practice, the chemical warfare training that a soldier on his way to France would undergo consisted of a mere hour or two of gas-defense lectures and a demonstration of how to wear a gas mask, if masks were available.[1]

The CSS personnel assigned to deploy chemical weapons on the Western Front were among the first members of the AEF to be sent to Europe, and they also needed to be trained. Arriving in January 1918, the CSS spent weeks training with Charles H. Foulkes and the members of the British Gas Service. One of the CSS officers in the group, J. B. Garlock, wrote that the British officers praised the Americans for their "keenness to learn and the rapidity with which they mastered the work."[2] Foulkes described the relationship with U.S. gas soldiers as "most cordial."[3] In addition to training the CSS, the British provided the organization with equipment such as masks, gas cylinders, mortars, and Livens projectors. Amos A. Fries, who served as director of the CSS in France during the war, said that all of the army's "equipment for gas troops came entirely from the English."[4]

Meanwhile, CSS instructors labored to provide the soldiers of the AEF with improved chemical warfare training in piecemeal fashion as they arrived in France. It was exciting work, constantly changing as instructional regimens were adjusted and upgraded. Officers and soldiers were sometimes trained and retrained as the CSS enhanced its training program. In July, gas-warfare training activities were centralized at the CSS's large laboratory complex and test range located outside Chaumont, called Experimental Field.[5] "I am particularly struck by the good nature of the fellows," wrote a CSS officer at the training center. "They are from most every division and are from all parts of United States. Some have never been to the front and others have been [at the front] over a year and more."[6]

CSS officers tried to train AEF soldiers how to identify different chemical weapons by sight and smell, and how to decontaminate themselves, their equipment, and their surroundings once chemical weapons were used. The CSS choreographed simulated gas attacks and taught soldiers how to put on their gas masks quickly and tighten them properly. They tried to encourage soldiers to wear their masks for hours at a time in order to acclimate them to the discomfort. Soldiers in training were even encouraged to play "Gas Baseball," a game that followed the standard rules of baseball, except that all the players were to wear their gas masks continuously during the game. Each game, however, was "to consist of not more than five innings and not to last more than two hours."[7]

A typical training schedule in mid-August consisted of six days of instruction and demonstrations, between 1:30 and 4:30 in the afternoon, and one simulated nighttime combat operation. Every day, a different variant of a gas-mask respirator exercise was conducted. On one day the men underwent mask training in a gas chamber. On another they went on a long hike in their protective gear. Besides mask drills, lectures were the most salient feature of the six-day training regime. CSS instructors lectured on the history of gas, development of gas warfare, offensive use of gas, gas defensive measures, and decontaminating procedures. They taught trainees how to inspect and maintain their masks and respirators, and also, incidentally, how to operate flamethrowers.[8] Class schedules from subsequent months show that gas training continued to cover the same subjects, and remained six days long, but trainees spent mornings as well as afternoons receiving instruction.

In addition to increasing the amount of time soldiers spent receiving gas training, CSS officers constantly strove to improve the quality of the lessons and exercises. Instructors at the training centers received regular updates about the fighting and information on new tactical developments in the battlefield use of gas in order to supplement the material they taught. They tried to make practical improvements as well. One week before the war ended, with not enough time to implement this particular innovation, a gas officer in the 4th Corps wrote a memorandum suggesting improvements to the standard military mask drill.[9] The drill was a series of steps taken to put on a gas mask, which soldiers repeated over and over during training so that donning a mask in combat would become second nature. In the memorandum, the officer pointed out that on an actual battlefield, soldiers do not usually put their masks on while standing up, as they are drilled to do. Most soldiers, the officer asserted, are under shell-fire when the gas alarm sounds and have already "hit the dirt" to avoid explosions and shrapnel.[10] He suggested that soldiers be taught to don masks while down on one knee or lying flat under cover.

Despite attempts to improve the quality of instruction over time, CSS training activities still fell short of what the soldiers in the army required. For example, in July 1918 Army Chief of Engineers William M. Black had to issue a notice about chemical training demonstrations:

> It has been noted that, in certain camps, demonstrations have been entirely too perfunctory, and entirely devoid of any characteristics which tend to make them appear at all realistic. There is no training value in a demonstration which is too obviously only a demonstration; it must have some of the characteristics, at least, of being real. It is of little value, for example, to open a cylinder of chlorine on the parade ground in order that a group of men in ranks may practice putting on masks; it is equally

valueless to stage a prepared cloud gas attack when the operators can be seen carrying up and turning on the cylinders. It is recommended that in all cases that so far as possible these demonstrations be carried out at night, at dusk, or preferably at dawn, and that all operations be concealed, allowing the surprise effect to the fullest extent.[11]

Gas-defense training also tended to vary from camp to camp, in spite of the existence of specific guidelines issued by the General Headquarters of the AEF. Such training fell considerably short of optimal. Perhaps the largest training discrepancy was in the area of artillery, however. No gas shells were allowed to be fired in training demonstrations, leaving CSS instructors little alternative but to describe artillery chemical attacks to trainees in classroom lectures.[12] Most of the chemical weapons used during the First World War were delivered by artillery shell, and American soldiers had no actual experience with the weapon before seeing it used against them on the battlefield.

Training an army of this size quickly and comprehensively was a monumental endeavor. Over the course of the war, a relative handful of CSS soldiers had to prepare an army of four million for the poisons they were going to encounter on the battlefield. Instructing the soldiers of the AEF was complicated by the fact that the generation had come of age before childhood education became universal across the United States, and a number of soldiers would have had little formal schooling. It was almost inevitable that some soldiers would be inadequately prepared. However, as the gas officer for the 33rd Division, W. E. Vawter, observed, "the most serious" obstacle the CSS encountered as it trained the AEF "was the imagination of the individual man."[13] In the absence of personal experience with poison gas, the soldiers of the AEF used their imagination, and that tendency led to dangerous misperceptions. "This feature," Vawter added, "accounted for too many gas casualties."[14] Gas clouds were terror weapons, capable of sowing confusion and damaging morale in excess of their ability to cause casualties. In a battlefield environment where small mistakes could get a person injured or killed, uncertainty about gas could cause casualties in and of itself.[15]

Accordingly, CSS trainers should have made it their priority to dispel chemical weapons myths and to assuage fears about poison gas shared by the soldiers. Unfortunately, this important responsibility was not appreciated until too late. CSS officers would admit that in their initial push to get American soldiers to understand the importance of gas-mask training, they may even have unintentionally intensified soldiers' anxiety about chemical weapons.

> An error in starting gas training inherited from our original advisors was to relate tales of suffering and agony of men who had been gassed, especially stories of men lightly gassed and who never expected any serious results, [and then] fell dead the following day after physical exertion. A certain percentage of men detecting gas in low concentrations began to think of all these stories and they were convinced that they were in a similar state of danger, so that there was only one thing to do, evacuate them. A respect of gas and not fear was being taught.[16]

After hearing these stories from CSS officers during training and then listening to the rumors and second-hand information traded among members of his unit, it is not surprising that the average American soldier was confused and uncertain when it came to poison gas. The doughboys improvised when they were unsure, and they made mistakes. Soldiers could believe that they sensed gas when there was none and waste unnecessary energy performing their duties in a gas mask. Other soldiers could want to avoid looking "green" in front of members of their unit and therefore wait too long to put their masks on. A soldier afraid of being gassed might leave his mask on for longer than necessary, exhaust the filter, and become vulnerable. Another soldier might believe incorrectly that invisible poison gas had dissipated and then take his mask off while dangerous fumes were still present.

In such an atmosphere, rumor and misinformation thrived. In May 1918 the CSS published a bulletin that cautioned soldiers in combat to keep their masks on until told to take them off "on the order of an officer known to them and who has his mask off when he gives the order." The reason given, almost certainly a rumor, was that "instances are known of the enemy's having sent over individuals during a gas attack for the purpose of ordering our troops to take off their masks."[17]

Gas paranoia was not a phenomena limited to enlisted men. Throughout World War I the CSS noted that AEF officers were reluctant to use poison gas offensively against the Germans. Commanders demonstrated an acute mistrust of poison gas, not only because they worried that the wind might blow the gas back onto American troops, but also because they feared that its use would instigate the Germans to retaliate in kind. CSS officers recorded the following (infamous) example:

> As illustrating some of these difficulties, the Assistant Chief of Staff, G-3 (Operations) of a certain American Corps refused to consider a recommendation to use gas on a certain point in the battle of the Argonne unless the gas officer would state in writing that if the gas was so used it could not possibly result in the casualty of a single American soldier. Such an attitude was perfectly absurd.[18]

It was the attitude of that officer, and many others like him, which prompted the CSS to act as ambassadors for chemical weapons in the AEF. In a statement that foreshadowed the public relations effort of the postwar period, CSS Colonel Richmond Mayo-Smith reportedly said that "Chemical Warfare Service officers have got to go out and sell gas to the Army."[19]

The CSS spent the First World War trying to convince their fellow soldiers that if they respected gas as a weapon, followed instructions, and used gas masks and other protective equipment, they could remain safe from enemy clouds. But for that conviction to ring true, the quality and utility of American gas masks would have to improve. The Department of War had decided to purchase and issue British small-box respirators (SBRs) after it became apparent that U.S. masks could not be manufactured in time. SBRs were reliable and had a filter that lasted many hours, but the soldiers found them extremely uncomfortable.[20] The straps that held the mask in place were reported to cause headaches. The SBR had a nose clip inside the rubber face piece that held your nostrils shut while you wore it. Breathing was accomplished through a hose with a mouthpiece that had to be held in place between your lips. Saliva tended to accumulate around it, and long periods of wear would irritate a soldier's lips and gums. The mask was so uncomfortable that in September 1918, officers in the CSS complained that "a rumor has reached this office that a few commanding officers are compelling men to wear the S. B. R. as punishment for minor offenses."[21] The CSS asked that this form of punishment end, "for it makes the men look upon the S. B. R. as an instrument of torture, and it may thus defeat the purpose for which the S. B. R. is intended."[22]

Assistant Secretary of War and Director of Munitions Benedict Crowell wrote that, in sum, "the word discomfort is a weak description of the feelings of a man wearing one of our masks for that period."[23] A more dangerous problem, however, was the tendency for moisture to dim, or fog, the eyepieces. "Reports from the war-front have indicated that the most serious difficulty in the modern gas mask, aside from its general discomfort, results from the moisture which collects on the eyepiece and obscures vision. In action the vision is often impaired that the soldier is compelled to lay aside his mask, or else lose efficiency as a fighter. If he chooses the former course, he can almost certainly be counted as a casualty."[24] As this Bureau of Mines report excerpt implies, the general discomfort of the mask and fogging of the eyepieces could cause the soldier to discard the mask at a critical moment and become vulnerable to poison gas.

The French-made Tissot mask was a good potential alternative to the British SBR for the Americans for several reasons: it fit comfortably over the face, did not have an uncomfortable nose or mouthpiece, and the lenses of the eyepieces did not fog up because of the way air flowed inside the mask. A pair of tubes inside the face piece blew air across the glass eyepieces as the soldier wearing it breathed. The principal is the same as a windshield defogger in a modern-day car. The U.S. government purchased very few Tissot masks, however, and they were distributed only to artillery units and medical personnel. The army believed that the face piece of the mask was too flimsy and the air valves too complex for standard infantry issue. Additionally, the Tissot mask's filter hung on the wearer's back instead of the front, making it unsuitable for any personnel who needed to carry packs or other equipment there.[25]

But because the SBR masks issued to American soldiers felt like torture devices, some doughboys improvised. U.S. soldiers sometimes procured French Army Tissot masks unofficially and used them in place of their regular masks. AEF commanders expressly forbade this practice because they believed it hurt morale: if soldiers saw their comrades opting for unauthorized equipment, misgivings about the safety of authorized gas masks might spread. Other soldiers engaged in a more dangerous practice: altering or misusing their masks to make them more comfortable to wear. The SBR was designed with extra material on both sides of the face piece so that wearers could manually wipe the inside of the eyepieces with the mask itself if the lenses fogged, but the extra material allowed the eyepieces to move around when the wearer was in motion, and constantly wiping the lenses by hand was tedious. Rather than suffer obscured vision, some soldiers had a "pernicious habit" of pulling the top part of the face piece down, exposing their eyes and forehead.[26] They believed, incorrectly, that they would be protected against gas as long as the nose clip and mouthpiece were in place.[27] Chemical weapons like mustard gas irritate the skin and eyes as well as the lungs, and leaving those areas exposed could result in chemical burns or blindness.

The problems with the SBR and Tissot masks lent necessity to the gas-mask development effort in the United States. Both the French and British masks had features that U.S. designers wanted to incorporate into a comfortable and sturdy prototype, but their early efforts were unsuccessful. At first the Bureau of Mines designed an American version of the SBR with an enhanced charcoal filter and a fuller face piece that made it easier for the wearer to clean the eyepieces, but the disadvantages of the mask outnumbered its advantages. The new filter was large and clumsy, making the American SBR heavier and more difficult to put on, and the new shape allowed the eyepiece lenses to fall out occasionally. Additionally, no improvements whatsoever were made to the uncomfortable mouth and nosepieces, and the eyepieces still fogged-up.[28] It was not until August 1918, nearly the end of the war, that improved American gas masks based on the French Tissot mask began to be designed and tested.[29] Two different masks, the Akron-Tissot mask and the Kops-Tissot mask, were created at the same time by different manufactures. Both American Tissot masks incorporated all of the benefits of the French version and featured improved strength and usability. Very few of these models were produced before the war ended, however.[30]

The soldiers of the AEF experienced problems with most types of gas-defensive equipment in addition to masks. An experimental substance called sag paste, for example, was an inert salve meant to be smeared over a soldier's entire body before going into combat to protect the skin against the effects of mustard gas, but the paste was uncomfortable to wear even in the best of circumstances. It also rubbed off on clothing and caked when the soldier perspired. More seriously, it did not neutralize the poison. If a soldier did not remove the paste from himself soon after being exposed, the mustard gas would be absorbed by the sag paste and make contact with the skin.[31] To treat soldiers who had been exposed to mustard gas, CSS Medical Director Harry L. Gilchrist ordered the construction of mobile degassing facilities for front-line divisions in June 1918. These degassing facilities were trucks that were intended to carry new clothes, medical supplies, a field shower, and a twelve-hundred-gallon tank of water with a heater to areas where soldiers had been contaminated by mustard gas. Only one such degassing unit was assembled by the end of the war, however, and it never saw front-line service.[32]

In an effort to minimize soldiers' contact with poison gas or prevent it altogether so that such treatments would not be necessary, the AEF initially purchased trench fans from the British, since those devices were widely used in their army. A trench fan was a flap of canvas attached to a wooden handle that soldiers would use to create an updraft in order to "shovel" gas clouds out of trenches and dugouts. But the doughboys found the use of the fans tedious and labor intensive, and their officers worried that manually swishing gas clouds around would cause exhaustion, lead to heavy breathing, and result in casualties. Trench fans eventually fell into disuse.[33] The AEF did have success using chloride of lime powder to decontaminate areas affected by mustard gas, but the substance could only be spread around relatively small areas and shell holes, and it was sometimes in short supply. Barrier methods such as gas-proof blankets were employed to protect entrances to dugouts in the trenches, to prevent gas from seeping down inside and poisoning the soldiers sheltering there. In many cases the chemically treated fabric was an effective protection method if it could be secured down over the entrance properly. A well-placed enemy artillery shell could rip the blanket off entirely, however, and there was some confusion among the soldiers about how the gas-proof fabric worked. "The principal of a gas-proof dug-out must be clearly explained to the men in the ranks as they are apt to get the idea that a gas-proof dug-out is ventilated in some mysterious way with pure air," the CSS lamented in May 1918. "As it really is, or should be, hermetically sealed, the importance of extinguishing fires immediately on letting down the curtain is evident."[34] The devices used to defend against poison gas during the First World War tended to be more effective in theory then they were in practice.

Other than the SBR, perhaps the most important piece of anti-gas equipment for the soldiers of the AEF was the gas alarm. A gas-warfare manual advised that "a local gas alarm must be fitted up at every sentry's post, occupied sap, battery position, etc., for the purpose of rousing men in the immediate vicinity and conveying warning to the sentries in charge of the long-distance gas alarms."[35] The alarm would alert soldiers within range of the gas to put on their masks before the fumes arrived, but supplying an alarm device that worked consistently well proved problematic. The ideal gas alarm needed to be loud enough to be heard amid the noise of battle and distinctive enough to avoid confusing it with other sounds. A false alarm would force men throughout the defensive line to spend hours awake in their gas masks while their officers tried to determine if any danger existed. Additionally, "no reliance can be placed on devices giving the alarm involving the use of the lungs—e.g., bugles or whistles," for reasons that should be obvious.[36] The CSS encouraged the use of an alarm device called a Strombos horn, which sounded a long, loud note when attached to a canister of compressed air, but they admitted that in practice "no standard pattern has been adopted for these local alarm devices. Klaxon horns, gongs (shell cases), large bells, 2-ft. lengths of steel rail or triangles made of steel rail and policemen's rattles . . . are all in use."[37]

In January 1918 the soldiers of the 1st Infantry Division became the first members of the AEF to occupy a position on the Western Front. Consequently, they became the first U.S. division to face chemical weapons in World War I. During the week that the 1st Infantry Division arrived, a neighboring French Army unit began moving hundreds of gas casualties from their front lines to hospitals in the rear, giving American soldiers their first sight of men wounded by chemical weapons.[38] The earliest recorded gas attack on the 1st Division occurred on February 2, but it was relatively insignificant. An estimated twenty-five gas artillery shells filled with a mixture of phosgene and diphosgene were fired at the 6th Field Artillery unit in a heavy afternoon fog near the town of Ansauville. As they had been trained, the men donned their gas masks when they heard the distinctive sound of the chemical shells "swish" and wobble through the air, but not one of the shells appeared to have exploded, and there were no casualties.[39] CSS officers, inexperienced and apprehensive, believed that the German shells employed some sort of delayed action fuse that would release the gas later. They dug up as many of the shells as they could find and collected them for analysis. It is likely that the fuses on the shells were simply faulty.

Four days later the German's lobbed a single, functioning, mustard-gas shell at the same artillery unit at Ansauville. As is typical of mustard gas, there were no immediate casualties; however, the 6th Field Artillery believed that they had sufficiently decontaminated the area with chloride of lime powder, so they remained there overnight. The next day the persistent chemical caused three soldiers in the unit to endure "severe conjunctivitis," and a fourth soldier suffered a "burned buttock."[40] In spite of the limited and uncoordinated nature of these first attacks, the first gas casualties in the AEF typified the challenge that mustard gas posed. U.S. soldiers would have more difficulty coping with mustard gas than any other chemical agent because of its ability to cause casualties long after it has been deployed.

Gas attacks with more severe consequences occurred not long after. The Germans launched their first Livens projector drums against the AEF in a wooded area at Bois de Remieres on February 26, heavily gassing elements of the 1st Division.[41] The attack happened around 1:00 A.M. and was accompanied by high-explosive mortar fire intended to cause additional confusion and panic. CSS officers believed that the gas used was a mixture of phosgene and tear gas, though descriptions from the soldiers, most of whom had never experienced a chemical attack before, varied. One account identified chlorine gas as having been used, another noted the smell of mustard gas, and there was also disagreement as to whether the tear gas used was chloropicrin or palite.[42]

Most of the soldiers in the gassed area were able to get their gas masks on in time, though some breathed in the gas while putting masks on and had to be treated later. Private Beddell of the 18th Infantry Division was on duty at a listening post when the gas exploded practically on top of him.[43] The force of the explosion knocked down a man beside him, and Beddell was gassed while trying to put a mask on the fallen man before he had put on his own. Private Liton, a telephone operator in the Signal Corps, managed to put his mask on in time after the concussion from the projector burst blew in the window and door of the dugout he was in, but another soldier in the dugout "went wild" with fright.[44] Liton and a lieutenant attempted to restrain the man and mask him, but Liton's gas mask was torn off in the struggle. Liton became injured by the gas as a result, and the man he attempted to assist died. Most of the division's casualties, however, were men who assumed that the gas dissipated long before it actually had and who removed their masks too soon. Approximately 225 U.S. soldiers of the 1st Division were in the vicinity during the attack and eighty-five of them, more than one-third, were injured or killed by the gas.[45] In the days before the attack, the Americans had noticed noisy hammering and other unusual activity associated with the construction of the Liven's projectors on the German side of no-man's-land, but the gas attack still managed to catch the 1st Division underprepared.[46]

Despite CSS training, the gas caused a substantial number of casualties within the division. Such episodes were unfortunately common in the AEF as the war continued and as more new soldiers from the United States continued to arrive. In World War I most American army units suffered a proportionately higher percentage of gas casualties in battle than their French, British, and even German counterparts. The 26th Infantry Division had the lamentable distinction of suffering the most gas casualties of any U.S. Army division in France. In two hundred days of front-line service, the 26th Division suffered 5,815 gas casualties, according to the Army Medical Department.[47]

Doctors and medics in uniform found that treating poison-gas casualties was more complicated than healing soldiers who had been wounded with more conventional weapons. During triage a physician would have to determine if a solder had been gassed, with what chemical, and how severely, based on observational evidence. The patients who suffered from genuine gas poisoning had to be distinguished from those who were experiencing gas fright or exhaustion. Soldiers who had been gassed could have residual chemicals on their bodies, clothing, or equipment. Particularly with mustard gas, there was a risk that the boots or the hair of an injured soldier could contaminate an entire hospital ward if precautions were not taken. CSS Medical Director Gilchrist recorded the following description of an ideal field dressing station operated in Bezu-le-Guery on July 1, 1918.

> When gas casualties occur they are immediately removed to the dressing station.... It occupies the church, adjoining school house, and two or three nearby buildings. It is divided into sections, the operating sec-

tion, dressing section, degassing section, and administrative section. Two tents have been erected adjoining a small building fitted up as a bath house, which are used for gassed casualties. Here they are stripped and assigned to the baths, those presenting serious symptoms are not permitted to get up but are bathed on litters in a reclining position; the others are marched into the bath house where they are given hot baths. The bath house is equipped with a portable heating apparatus connected with six shower heads. After the men have been bathed and dried, their eyes, noses and throats are sprayed with a solution of bicarbonate of soda, following which they are dressed in pajamas and removed to the church which is fitted up as a temporary hospital. From here, they are evacuated to the special gas hospital at Luzancy as soon as possible.[48]

It was hoped that cleaning the patients thoroughly at the dressing station would prevent the contamination of other patients and staff during treatment and convalescence, but not all medical stations were as well situated as this one at Bézu-le-Guéry. Battalion-level aid stations were improvised in a variety of locations near the fighting front, such as abandoned cellars and dugouts.[49] Aid-station personnel were constantly exposed to poison fumes from the chemical casualties in small, poorly ventilated areas, and there was usually a shortage of water for cleaning the patients. The staff would have to conserve the available resources by deciding how thoroughly or not to bathe a soldier before transferring him to a more permanent hospital away from the front. Gassed patients were transported in separate ambulances from other wounded whenever possible.[50] Once they arrived at a gas hospital, wounded soldiers could expect a long period of recovery, depending on the severity of their injuries. Soldiers had to wait until they regained sufficient lung function to perform their duties. Mustard gas patients usually took longer to recover than other wounded, and they usually experienced a greater variety of injuries including blindness, burns, and gastro-intestinal problems.

As more new American divisions moved into defensive positions on the Western Front through the winter, the Germans planned their spring offensive to take advantage of the U.S. Army's small numbers and relative inexperience. During the Ludendorff Offensive, which lasted from March to July 1918, the AEF aided in the defense of far-flung French villages throughout the front, places like Epernay, Cantigny, Meteren, and many others. The French, British, and U.S. forces ultimately prevailed, but the intensity and duration of the fighting represented a trial by fire for the American newcomers.

In some cases the doughboys demonstrated good gas discipline and successfully defended against chemical attack with minimal casualties.

A medical officer named Eugene A. Curtin wrote in a letter home on April 15, "We have had no lack of excitement since the old Hun started in to muss up the world in general on the 21st of March." He continued, "A few days before the Hun orchestra started the overture with gas and we all got some of it, myself included. While it did not lay us out, due to the continual use of our masks, we nevertheless got enough of it to make us miserable."[51] Though Curtin sustained no permanent injury and soon returned to his unit, gas was a capricious weapon with an ability to produce casualties that varied from circumstance to circumstance, and not everyone was so fortunate.

The U.S. Army 2nd Division helped defend an area of trenches near Saint-Mihiel during the spring offensive and, from April 6 through April 13, they sustained several heavy phosgene and mustard-gas attacks and suffered many casualties. All U.S. corps, divisions, and regiments were assigned gas officers from the CSS, who were responsible for advising commanders about chemical weapons, supervising gas defensive operations, maintaining anti-gas equipment, and conducting gas training.[52] In his report following the attacks, the gas officer for the 2nd Division expressed frustration about how poorly the soldiers were faring. "The number of casualties was inexcusably large, 277 being evacuated up until noon of April 14th," he wrote. "Of these all suffered from conjunctivitis, many having infected lungs and several are badly blistered."[53] Together with the experiences of the 1st Division and other Army units, this battle added to the growing mountain of evidence that the AEF was vulnerable to poison-gas attacks. CSS officers began to face the implication that the bulk of the U.S. Army was badly suited to defend itself against chemical weapons.

The CSS and the 2nd Division attempted to blame each other for the heavy casualties. The division's officers claimed that the CSS had failed to properly train and equip their soldiers, while the gas officers claimed that the soldiers and their commanders had not taken defensive measures seriously.[54] Both accusations were probably true. Throughout World War I, division and regimental gas officers worked to identify the causes of gas casualties with the hope of making soldiers safer in future attacks; however, their investigations often ended in finger pointing.

The victims of chemical attacks themselves were frequently blamed for becoming gas casualties because they failed to don their masks quickly enough or to keep them on long enough for the gas to dissipate. In a few cases the French were held responsible for American casualties. After a minor chemical attack on an artillery unit in the 42nd Division caused forty-five casualties in March 1918, the gas officer concluded that the wounded "were the result of the Officer in charge taking the word of a

French Lieutenant who told him the gas wasn't strong enough to do any damage."[55] Another gas officer attributed nearly two hundred casualties suffered by the 77th Division during a mustard-gas attack on June 24 "due to the fact that the *French N.C.Os stated that there was no gas present*" and U.S. soldiers had removed their masks prematurely. "I recommend," he wrote, "that a special order be sent out to all units that our men must not remove their masks on orders from the French. On investigation, I learned that it was common for the men of the 42nd Division to complain of the French telling them to remove their masks, and on doing so to find gas present."[56]

AEF officers were also often blamed for failing to enforce adequate protective measures during gas attacks, as had happened with the 2nd Division at Saint-Mihiel. When the 18th Infantry Regiment suffered a staggering 693 casualties during a gas attack in May, the largest share of the blame fell on the regiment's gas officer, Lieutenant Robert A. Hall, who was alleged to have neglected his duties before and during the attack. Among other accusations, Hall was seen wearing the French Tissot gas mask instead of the CSS-approved British SBR. According to the CSS officer who investigated the incident, when Hall wore the more comfortable French mask, it caused a great deal of confusion in the regiment about which type of mask to wear during the attack. Some soldiers switched masks while potent gas fumes still lingered in the air, and other soldiers neglected to wear the SBR at all.[57] The actions of Hall and the other officers of the 18th Infantry were deemed "contrary to existing orders, and highly detrimental to gas discipline," and it was ultimately recommended that Hall be relieved of his duties and reassigned.[58] Hall may have been culpable in this instance, but the CSS had an unfortunate tendency to attribute gas casualties to individuals and circumstances instead of blaming inadequate training, poor defensive procedures, or deficient equipment.

While working to improve the AEF's ability to defend itself against chemical attacks in the spring and early summer, the CSS also worked to accomplish its offensive mandate and use gas as a weapon against the enemy. The combat backbone of the CSS was a unit from the Corps of Engineers, called the 30th Engineers, commanded by Earl J. Atkisson. Though many members of the unit had professional backgrounds in chemistry and chemical engineering, they had no practical experience deploying poison gas on the battlefield until they completed their training with the British and practiced their first offensive action on the evening of June 18, 1918. Their targets were German encampments around La Ferme Saint Marie, west of Pont-à-Mousson, where there were three enemy companies and a battalion headquarters. Since the purpose of the action was to train the American gas soldiers, it took place in an area of very little fighting, described as "the most peaceful of all 'peace-time' fronts."⁵⁹ To carry out the attack, the 30th Engineers, with the support of the U.S. Army 26th Division, installed nineteen hundred Livens projectors less than a mile from the German encampments.

The 30th Engineers suffered no casualties as they prepared and installed the projectors. At the appointed hour, the Livens projectors launched smoke clouds and phosgene gas at their targets in sequence, while French Army artillery pieces simultaneously bombarded the Germans at La Ferme Saint Marie. Approximately ten minutes after the initial attack, German artillery pieces began to shell the 26th Division in retaliation. The counterattack lasted for several hours, but no gas soldiers in the 30th Engineers were killed or wounded. The gas soldiers conducted a withdrawal from the fighting front, under the artillery fire, once the Livens projectors had been discharged and their mission completed.⁶⁰

It was difficult to judge how effective the first U.S. gas attack had been, because gauging the effectiveness of chemical weapons in general was complicated by several factors. Armies rarely followed up a poison gas attack with reconnaissance or an infantry assault into the area, because lingering chemical fumes would have posed a danger to them. Except in rare cases where masked soldiers personally reconnoitered a gassed enemy area, the CSS relied on a host of indirect evidence to estimate the effectiveness of its attacks. In this case the intensity of the German counterattack convinced the gas regiment that the casualties they had caused among the Germans had been significant. They also relied on subsequent prisoner interrogations, which determined that the German units targeted by the gas were being relieved by another division at the time of the attack. That would tend to increase the number of German casualties. Poison gas was estimated to have caused at least ten deaths and thirty injuries in one German company alone.⁶¹ The 30th Engineers considered their first action a success, and they anticipated many more such successes in the future, but the rest of the AEF viewed this gas attack differently. They took into consideration the fact that the gas soldiers had turned a peaceful front into an artillery duel. The duration and strength of the German retaliation suggested that in the future the Germans would respond to large chemical attacks with ferocity. Some army officers felt that the artillery bombardment experienced by the 26th Division as a result of this attack was not worth the damage that had been done to the enemy.⁶²

Accordingly, the 30th Engineers spent the next month virtually sidelined as the AEF participated in a large-scale offensive along the Marne River northeast of Paris, at Château-Thierry and Belleau Wood. The battle involved almost three hundred thousand American soldiers and was the single largest U.S. contribution to the fighting so far. The 30th Engineers were initially ordered to take part in the July offensive at Château-Thierry, but once they arrived they were ordered to perform unrelated duties. The soldiers were told that the fighting front was moving forward too rapidly for gas attacks to be practical, but James Thayer Addison, the chaplain of the 30th Engineers, wrote that the decision was also made "partly because plans for gas warfare seemed to many to be novel and even trivial."[63] Deprived of their regular duties, the soldiers of the 30th Engineers proved versatile. The men served as road-repair crews and burial parties; they created smoke screens to mask troop movements and even fired cannons of propaganda leaflets over the battlefield urging Germans to foster social revolution and end the war, although the soldiers "naturally chafed at the lack of opportunities for which they had so long and so carefully been trained."[64] The Germans were ultimately driven back from the Marne River after several weeks of fighting, and the Allies halted the offensive to begin preparing for another one at Saint-Mihiel.

The Château-Thierry offensive ended without the 30th Engineers launching any chemical weapons, but poison gas was used by the AEF nevertheless. U.S. artillery units fired gas shells during the fighting, independent of the soldiers in the gas regiment. Throughout World War I, the AEF favored chemical-weapons delivery systems that discharged smaller quantities of gas instead of the larger-scale Livens projector attacks for which the 30th Engineers were equipped. An estimated 85 percent of all poison gas used in the First World War was delivered by artillery and mortar shell.[65] While a Livens projector burst briefly saturates the target area in poison chemicals, firing individual shells repeatedly at the same location would instead allow the AEF to maintain a lower concentration of gas for longer periods. Projectors depended on the element of surprise to catch enemy soldiers who were unable to don their masks quickly enough, but a steady hail of gas shells could force them to work in hazardous conditions for hours.

American artillerists chiefly used phosgene and mustard gas shells and avoided the use of visible smoke. Most French artillery shells contained smoke-generating chemicals as well as toxic gas; this allowed artillerists to see the gas clouds forming over the enemy's position and to adjust their fire as needed. Americans preferred instead to use artillery shells that were completely filled with poison gas in order to maximize their effectiveness and to keep the gas cloud invisible to the enemy.[66] CSS officer Ernest McCullough described a typical attack and its intended results.

The usual practice towards the end of the war was to put up a two-minute burst of fire with toxic shells donning immediate effect and to follow this with a long, continued fire of more persistent gasses. The continuous fire was varied from time to time with short bursts of toxic gasses in order to catch men who had removed their masks from time to time to get relief, or to penetrate canisters which had become defective.[67]

Of course, wearing a gas mask for an extended period is uncomfortable and demoralizing, and if the mask malfunctioned or the filter wore out, the soldier wearing it could become a casualty. To increase confusion and panic, artillery units could also alternate between firing poison gas shells and shells filled with shrapnel or lacrimony agents. If enemy soldiers ultimately evacuated the gassed area and the artillery ceased shelling, the low concentration could dissipate relatively quickly and allow the AEF to occupy the enemy position sooner.

The AEF's "Instructions for the Use of Chemical Shells by Artillery," which was prepared in January 1918 based on information from the British and the French, listed eight types of targets for which artillerists should employ gas shells: "Villages in which enemy troops are quartered, groups of dug-outs anywhere, areas where enemy troops are being concentrated or where it is desirable to prevent the assembly of enemy troops, lines of communication, machine gun emplacements, battery positions, and positions beyond the objective being attacked by our troops or on the flanking side of a proposed infantry attack, and *all working parties.*"[68]

In contrast, McCullough's study of gas artillery shells, produced after the CSS had experienced chemical warfare in battle for itself, consolidated and simplified the list into three types of artillery fire: harassing, neutralization, and interdiction.[69] Harassing fire was used to gas roads and rear areas where enemy soldiers tended to congregate. Neutralization fire was used against enemy artillery positions, and it would force the gassed gun crews to evacuate the area and reposition their weapons. Interdiction fire used persistent gasses to deny the enemy use of roads and bridges during an advance or attack. The targets that McCullough described would all have been relatively deep inside an enemy area, where the wind would be unlikely to blow the gas back toward friendly soldiers, and soldiers who advanced into front line enemy positions would not have to fight in areas gassed by their own artillery.

The use of gas shells by artillery presented several serious difficulties. Gas warfare required artillerists to remain mindful of terrain and weather conditions, because environmental factors affect the concentration, persistency, and lethality of poison gas. The "Instructions for the

Use of Chemical Shells by Artillery" explained that "the effective use of gas shells is much more dependent upon weather conditions than is the case with other forms of projectiles. Wind direction and velocity, temperature, humidity, and nature of ground are all important factors which must be considered."[70]

> Wind direction is of prime importance and great care must be taken in choosing targets for gas shells when the wind is blowing *towards* our own lines. An extremely hot sun is detrimental to the effectiveness of gas because it causes the shell contents to be vaporized too rapidly and ascending air currents dissipate the gas. On the other hand, extreme cold delays vaporization. A moist atmosphere is desirable, though a *heavy rain* diminishes the effectiveness of gas attacks. On the whole, ideal weather conditions (absence of wind, moderately high temperature, and moist atmosphere) usually occur on a summer night. Their effect is greatest in places that are sheltered from the wind such as woods, valleys, closely built villages or ground covered with thick brush.[71]

Artillery crews in the AEF had to understand a great deal about how prevailing conditions would affect the gasses they used, but that was not the only unique challenge that chemical weapons presented. Different types of gas shells were marked with symbols or bands of colored paint to indicate which chemical mixture was inside. Overall this identification system worked poorly. The shells and the gasses they were filled with came from factories across the United States, Britain, and France, and standardization proved extremely difficult. In practice, artillerists had to memorize an ever-changing list of identifying marks if they hoped (for example) to launch a barrage of smoke and white phosphorous and not mustard gas. Artillerists who fired gas shells also did so under the threat of retaliation in kind. Gun crews wore their gas masks constantly, not only out of fear of German gas attack but also because their own gas shells would sometimes leak. "Leaking gas shells can best be disposed of by firing from the gun," the soldiers were advised, "If the condition of the shell is such that [firing] is impossible, it should be buried under at least 5 feet of earth."[72] In recognition of the fact that SBR gas masks were too uncomfortable to be worn for these extended periods, doughboys in AEF artillery units were permitted to wear the French Tissot mask instead.[73]

In light of the many difficulties the AEF was experiencing with respect to using and defending against poison gas in France, the CSS pushed the Department of War harder to undertake a major restructuring of the U.S. chemical warfare program through the summer of 1918. CSS officers were led by a newly appointed director in Washington, D.C., Major General William L. Sibert. At the outset of World War I in 1917, Sibert had initially been appointed to command the 1st Division of the U.S. Army in France. After a short time in this relatively prominent position, however, the commander of the AEF, John J. Pershing, removed Sibert for poor performance and sent him back to the United States to lead the Gas Service.[74] Once he arrived in that position, Sibert worked with fellow CSS officers to coordinate the disparate gas-warfare responsibilities vested with the Bureau of Mines, Surgeon General's Office, and Ordnance Department. They believed that centralizing all chemical warfare activities into one, consolidated, Chemical Warfare Service would streamline administration and communication, allow the United States to manufacture more gas and related equipment, and also improve the AEF's ability to defend itself against German gas in France. With the AEF almost entirely dependent on gas equipment manufactured in France and Britain, and with its soldiers suffering a proportionally higher number of gas casualties than their allies or their enemies, the Department of War was willing to implement CSS recommendations that seemed capable of improving conditions.

While it was possible for the Department of War to consolidate the various gas activities within army agencies, the Bureau of Mines was a civilian agency within the Department of the Interior. An order from the President of the United States would be required to reassign resources from one cabinet agency to another. Convincing President Woodrow Wilson to change the existing administrative arrangement would be problematic, however, because all agreed that the Bureau of Mines had been doing excellent work under difficult circumstances. Sibert and the officers of the CSS simply believed that a more centralized research organization, operating from within the military, would operate more effectively. That assertion touched on a larger fundamental question about the nature of research and scientific discovery. Who should conduct scientific research vital to national defense: civilians or soldiers? Soldier-chemists could work efficiently within the military, and they could be trusted to keep their work secret, but would the army command structure and intellectual isolation make scientific discoveries less likely? Conversely, the intellectual exchange and free flow of ideas essential to scientific discovery could better occur among civilian chemists, but would that intellectual openness cause a security risk, and did civilian scientists work less efficiently than military ones?

The Department of the Interior and the Department of War exchanged memoranda about transferring chemical warfare responsibilities away from the Bureau of Mines throughout the first half of 1918. On May 15, 1918, Secretary of the Interior Franklin K. Lane wrote to President Wilson directly and asked him to prevent the proposed reorganization. "It would be a great mistake," Lane wrote about the Gas Investigations Division at the Bureau of Mines, "to take this out of civilian hands."[75] Wilson's reply professed ignorance of the subject and requested more information.

On May 16, a group of chemists who worked with the Bureau of Mines sent Lane a letter encouraging his opposition of the Department of War's consolidation plan. The group included William H. Nichols, a leader of the American Chemical Society, which was the largest professional association of chemists in the United States. Nichols and his group later wrote that they opposed the transfer because the work the Bureau of Mines was doing was competent and innovative. "We believed also," they said, "that the spirit of the Bureau of Mines was through its very nature more conductive to research than that of the War Department, the strictly military division of the Government. Then, too, we feared the numbing effect of the much discussed 'red tape' of War Department methods upon the spirit of originality, daring and speed in following new trails, so essential to the successful prosecution of research."[76] In the face of this opposition, the Department of War formerly asked the Secretary of the Interior to transfer the chemical warfare activities of the Bureau of Mines to a new chemical warfare division under its authority on May 21, 1918.

A meeting was held in Secretary of War Newton Baker's office on the afternoon of May 25 to discuss the transfer and allow the opposing parties to articulate their respective positions. The members of the Department of War who attended were Baker, Crowell, Army Chief of Staff Peyton C. March, Sibert, and CSS officers Marston T. Bogert and William S. Bacon. Lane was traveling outside the country, but First Assistant Secretary of the Interior Alexander Vogelsang attended in his place, along with Van H. Manning and George A. Burrell from the Bureau of Mines.[77]

Manning spent some time at the start of the meeting expounding the chemical weapons work undertaken by the Bureau of Mines and lauding the organization's achievements. He asserted that the Bureau of Mines should continue to perform chemical weapons research because it had a proven record of success in the field. Sibert responded that the issue was one of "control, that more efficiency could be secured by direct authority than by cooperation."[78] Manning disputed this point, saying that "more efficient work could be done by a research organization by leaving it out of military organization, because technical and scientific men would work better by request than order."[79] Manning feared the regimentation and "red tape" that Nichols and other chemists thought an army organization would engender. The meeting ended after two hours with no resolution, but Baker and Vogelsang spoke with each other privately immediately afterward. Baker indicated that he was not yet persuaded that the proposed transfer would be beneficial, and he promised Vogelsang "that he would try to convince General Sibert that the present arrangement should be continued."[80]

In a telegram from France on June 3, Pershing recommended to March that chemical warfare work be consolidated into one organization. He wrote that poison gas "may have great influence in securing ultimate victory," and that "it is therefore requested that the President direct that in view of the existing emergency there be established in the National Army a Gas Corps."[81] Such a request from Pershing certainly carried weight. On June 25, Baker wrote to President Wilson officially recommending the transfer of Manning's organization to Sibert. In spite of his recommendation, Baker commended Manning and the Bureau of Mines.

> In the early days of preparation and organization, Dr. Manning's contact with scientific men throughout the country was immensely valuable. He was able to summon from the universities and the technical laboratories of the country men of the highest quality and to inspire them with enthusiastic zeal in attacking new and difficult problems which had to be solved with the utmost speed. I do not see how the work could have been better done than he did it, and the present suggestion that the section now pass under the direction and control of the War Department grows out of the fact that the whole subject of gas warfare has assumed a fresh pressure and intensity, and the director of it must have the widest control so as to be able to use the resources at his command in the most effective way possible.[82]

Wilson approved the recommendation and issued an executive order authorizing the transfer that same day.[83] The consolidation of all gas warfare activities in the Department of War and the Bureau of Mines became effective on June 29, 1918, under the Overman Act, recently passed legislation that gave the president the power to coordinate government agencies in wartime. All of the twelve hundred civilian employees and the six hundred commissioned and noncommissioned men of the Bureau of Mines Gas Investigations Division were transferred to the soon-to-be-named Chemical Warfare Service (CWS) of the U.S. Army. The chemical warfare duties of the Surgeon General's Office, the Ordnance Department, and the Corps of Engineers were all also consolidated into the CWS.

Manning sent letters to Wilson and Sibert that acknowledged the transfer and then mailed copies of Wilson's order and Baker's letter to dozens of people involved in the work of the Bureau of Mines and to members of Congress over the next several days.[84] He forwarded the letters from Baker and President Wilson to Charles H. Herty, editor of the chemical industry periodical *Journal of Industrial and Engineering Chemistry;* Manning asked Herty to bring the letters to the attention of the *New York Times* as well. Herty's journal and other chemical industry periodicals reprinted the letters in full.[85] In the aftermath of Wilson's executive order, Manning managed to spread the word that the transfer was not the result of any negligence or failure at the Department of the Interior, and he tried to ensure that the chemists and other personnel of the Gas Investigations Division received recognition for all that they had accomplished. Individuals in the scientific community wrote letters of condolence to Manning, but industry periodicals generally viewed the transfer as a sign that the Department of War was acknowledging the important role of chemists in the war effort.[86]

Confronted with a chemical warfare crisis on the battlefield in France, the military's decision to assume responsibility for research related to chemical weapons may have been a good one in the long run. Nevertheless, the civilians who worked with the Bureau of Mines correctly asserted that scientific discovery can flourish in an unfettered atmosphere of intellectual and administrative independence. Not only is it possible that the U.S. chemical warfare program suffered when it was placed solely under military authority, but the timing of the transfer was also particularly poor. When the CWS assumed responsibility for chemical weapons research in June, there were only five months of fighting remaining before the war would end in November. Had anyone known that the First World War would end relatively soon, the Bureau of Mines could have been left to continue poison-gas research uninterrupted. Instead, valuable time and resources were wasted as officers and civilian personnel adjusted to their new organization and working relationships.

Once the CWS won control of chemical weapons research from the Bureau of Mines, its officers began to implement policies designed to court chemists. They allowed most of the chemists who had worked for the Bureau of Mines to continue to work as civilians within the CWS. A notable exception was George A. Burrell, head of the Gas Investigations Division, who was put into uniform as a colonel. The CWS also worked to locate and transfer chemists who were scattered around in various other areas of the army. When the military draft was first instituted in May 1917, there were no exemptions for chemists, and the army compounded this oversight by putting drafted chemists into the general pool of soldiers eligible for frontline service. Chemists believed that they should be a protected class of specialists, and they protested both of these practices.[87] Prominent organic chemist and CWS officer

Marston T. Bogert wrote that "the sending of chemists to the line in a war which can most accurately be described as a chemical war, was a suicidal blunder."[88] The CWS earned the thanks of chemists nationwide by raising awareness within the Department of War about the important war-related skills that chemists possessed, and by working to secure for them military assignments where they could use their training.

The CWS also assumed administration of Edgewood Arsenal, Maryland, from the Ordnance Department and continued the rapid expansion of its facilities under the direction of Colonel William H. Walker. Poison-gas factories and support buildings were already under construction around the shell-filling plant that had been built there in 1917. The erection of a large chloropicrin plant began at Edgewood on January 25, 1918. Chloropicrin was a powerful tear gas that was sometimes used on its own and sometimes mixed with other war gasses to make them more irritating. Once it was completed, the plant housed ten enormous chloropicrin stills, each eight feet wide and eighteen feet tall.[89] In March the army also began building a lethal-gas plant, designed particularly to manufacture phosgene. Phosgene is very sensitive to heat and cold, so the temperature of the chemical reactions had to be carefully controlled at every stage of the manufacturing process. Refrigeration units kept the gas in liquid form so that it could be poured into artillery shells that were cooled to 0 degrees Fahrenheit.[90] By the end of World War I, the phosgene plant could produce forty tons of the gas per day, and a "practically completed" expansion was ready to double that capacity.[91]

By July 1918 the shell-filling, chloropicrin, and phosgene plants were all operational, and construction at Edgewood continued to abound.[92] Contemporaries marveled at the grand scale of the place. *Scientific American* reported that "in considerably less than 12 months of active construction, we [the United States] built from the ground up a vast establishment, and developed an industry entirely new to the United States."[93] The chemists and engineers at Edgewood erected a research lab, a power station, a water system, warehouses, rail spurs, officers' quarters, worker barracks, and a thirty-four-building hospital capable of treating 420 patients. The CWS recorded that by October 1, 1918, the arsenal teemed with a population of 233 officers, 6,948 enlisted men, and 3,066 civilians.[94] *Scientific American* concluded, "We do not recall any other governmental work which surpasses this in the intelligent prevision with which it was laid out, the speed with which it was erected, and the brief period of time in which production on a large scale was accomplished."[95]

The Ordnance Department made the decision to build a chlorine gas plant at Edgewood in winter 1917 because, in the words of one of the plant's designers, "chlorine is the base from which practically every gas is made which is used in warfare."[96] Over time, the plans for the facility expanded in size and scope, but construction did not begin until the summer that the CWS formally took over administration of Edgewood. Lieutenant Colonel E. B. Ellicott of the Department of War Construction Division, plant designers H. R. Nelson and Samuel M. Green, and a large team of engineers erected two cavernous buildings, each filled with rows of hundreds of electrolytic chlorine cells, as well as several additional buildings to house the other aspects of the manufacturing process. An estimated two hundred tons of salt per day would be needed for the plant to operate at capacity, so a rail spur was built for salt trains to unload directly into several large vats at the brine facility. An auxiliary power plant had to be built to supply the factory's anticipated electrical needs. A system of pipes that ran along an elevated truss more than twenty-four hundred feet long was also built to pump the gas to other plants that needed it. This manufacturing complex was only partially online by the November armistice, but if it had reached peak production, this unprecedented facility, the CWS estimated, would have had the largest capacity of any chlorine gas factory in the world.[97]

Not all of the accomplishments at Edgewood were as celebrated. In May the army began the construction of a mustard-gas plant at Edgewood Arsenal, which would employ the method of manufacture created by James B. Conant and developed by Frank M. Dorsey of the Gas Investigations Division.[98] Since it was a new production method, the equipment and procedures for making mustard gas were not well tested or established. Captain H. H. Hanson, the officer in charge of constructing and operating the mustard-gas plant at Edgewood, and his staff of engineers had to design and build much of the equipment themselves. In order to produce mustard gas, they first had to innovate a way to manufacture large quantities of ethylene. The forty specially designed kaolin reactors they constructed were capable of producing sixteen thousand cubic feet of ethylene per hour and were called "one of the engineering triumphs of Edgewood."[99] Hanson and his officers also built thirty large reactors to produce the sulfur monochloride that would be needed in the mustard-gas manufacturing process.

The ethylene and sulfur monochloride were combined in experimental mustard reactors to produce the liquid mustard gas, but very serious problems occurred at this step. These reactors were specially designed lead tanks filled with coils of pipe through which brine or cold water would flow in order to control the temperature of the chemical reaction. While the first experimental mustard reactors built at Edgewood were able to produce large quantities of the liquid initially, they had to be shut down after a few days of operation. The reactor tanks and pipes had filled with sulfur waste, described as being "of a consistency of chewing gum," and there had also been problems with the ethylene injector nozzles becoming clogged inside the tank.[100] William B. Loach, an operator at the mustard-gas factory, estimated that for every pound of liquid mustard gas they made, a fifth of a pound of sulfur was also produced.[101] At that rate, the reactors had quickly filled with solid sulfur waste and become inoperable.

"When making ordinary chemicals," Loach said, "such a system can be cleaned out, but not with 'mustard.'"[102] The waste sulfur inside the reactors was completely saturated with mustard gas, and the solid clumps proved impossible to remove remotely. At first the designers tried flooding the tanks with cleaning solvent to wash out the residual sulfur, but this process failed to dislocate the stubborn chunks of toxic waste. The alternative was to clean out the reactors more or less by hand, but the gas made everything inside the reactor unsafe. CWS officers indicated that "it is almost impossible to economically remove [the residual gas], and its presence adds to the difficulty of removing the sulfur from the reactors; the men engaged in this operation almost always become casualties."[103]

The engineers quickly built twenty new and improved mustard-gas reactors of various designs at the factory through the summer of 1918, but all of them had similar problems. "At no time was it possible," Loach bemoaned, "because of troubles without number, to run more than 5 reactors in this plant at once."[104] The more mustard gas the reactors produced, the more solid sulfur was left inside the reactors. The sulfur sat at the bottom of the tanks, taking up more and more space. It caked onto the cooling coils, making it impossible to regulate the exothermic reaction; it clogged up the pipes, causing stoppages and leaks. Ambient conditions inside the mustard-gas plant were terrible. Even with only some of the mustard gas tanks operational, the chemical reactions inside them produced temperatures around one hundred degrees inside the factory. The "nauseating and burning fumes" of the mustard gas were "always in the air," sickening and injuring the soldiers who worked there.[105] Hanson lamented that for the workers the "danger of serious injuries was always present, yet there was no respite except the hospital."[106] There were no civilians who were willing to work in the mustard-gas plant, so even the most mundane tasks were dependent on enlisted personnel and officers. Since injuries were common and few men were willing to do the work, those left behind to operate the plant often had to work long shifts with little rest. Worst of all, every few days the inside of the reactors would have to be cleaned, and everyone knew that "it was in the removal of precipitated sulfur that most of our casualties occurred."[107]

The workforce at the mustard-gas factory suffered a staggering 674 casualties during the seven months the plant was in operation.[108] While work in all of the poison gas plants was hazardous, there were only 251 casualties in all of the other factories at Edgewood combined during the same period. The second most hazardous Edgewood plant was the massive chlorine factory, responsible for only sixty-two injuries.[109] The number of mustard-gas casualties is shocking, particularly considering that the plant never reached full production and was regularly inactive for long periods while the operators worked to make the process safer. When the postwar chief of the CWS, Amos A. Fries, told a Senate committee in 1919 that "everybody we put in that building got burned," he was not using hyperbole.[110]

Like most of the factories at Edgewood Arsenal, the mustard-gas plant had been grand in its conception. Originally commissioned to produce fifty tons of mustard gas per day, its full production potential was more than twice that by the end of World War I.[111] And despite the frequent equipment failures and accidents that occurred at Edgewood, the plant reportedly still managed to manufacture, on average, more mustard gas per day than both the British and French produced per month.[112] After the war ended, the CWS learned that the entire German chemical industry had been able to manage a collective production rate of only six tons of mustard gas per day.

The relatively large capacities of the mustard-gas plant and the other chemical-weapons facilities at Edgewood may seem excessive. However, the officers of the CWS believed that the chemical metropolis they had constructed would be needed to supply an expanding war effort of indefinite duration, where poison gas would play an essential part. The unfortunate irony was that Edgewood Arsenal did not manage to produce and ship enough chemical weapons to supply the AEF before the war ended in November. Construction schedules, shipping delays, and material shortages made the U.S. Army dependent on French and British chemical warfare equipment, and the AEF did not fire a single poison gas shell filled at Edgewood during the First World War. At a 1920 hearing on war expenditures in the House of Representatives, Fries reflected on their failure to supply the AEF despite the vast production capabilities that were being developed at Edgewood: "I have felt that one trouble was we started on too great a scale. In other words, we started to build an enormous skyscraper for making shells, on such a plan that we could not get a single shell finished until we got the whole skyscraper system working."[113] Fries explained that a number of scattered, smaller-scale manufacturing operations would have allowed more chemical warfare supplies to be produced in the United States more quickly in the short term, but he asserted that if the war had lasted longer, Edgewood Arsenal would have reached full productive ability.[114]

While CWS soldiers in the United States were fighting the "Battle of Edgewood," their counterparts in France, for the most part, remained sidelined. AEF gas officers continued their training and inspection duties, but the battlefield use of gas was largely limited to U.S. artillery units instead of the 30th Engineers. On May 31 an early-morning trench raid performed by the 101st Infantry Regiment went tragically wrong when the wind blew American gas back on to the advancing soldiers. The 101st and 103rd Artillery Regiments in the 26th Division, as well as some French artillery units, were ordered to support the raid by firing a box barrage around a segment of trenches near Lahayville while simultaneously saturating the town with more than sixteen hundred phosgene shells. A strong, steady wind blew the gas back toward the three hundred raiding AEF soldiers, causing 236 casualties. Evidently, none of the artillery batteries involved were aware of the wind speed or direction when the attack commenced, and none of the gas officers in the 26th Division were consulted about the use of gas.[115] Incidents like this were prima facie evidence that careless mistakes were causing gas casualties, and such events were galling to the CWS, whose experts had gone unutilized.

The 30th Engineers experienced their first combat fatalities on June 30, when they fell under German artillery fire while conducting a conventional mortar attack. Among those killed was an officer, 2nd Lieutenant Joseph T. Hanlon, whom the 30th Engineers mourned deeply.[116] He was eulogized as "an officer of unusual promise, great ability, high ideals, every inch a soldier and one who was loved by all who knew him."[117] "In his death," it was said, "the Service suffered a serious loss."[118] The CWS's training ground in France, Experimental Field, was renamed Hanlon Field in his honor.

In August, the 30th Engineers began receiving new orders to deploy chemical weapons against the Germans in several places along the Western Front. One of the largest operations took place in the Vosges Sector near the town of Rambervillers. The French had observed new trench construction in the German lines near a hill under French control, called Tête du Violu, and they suspected that the Germans were planning to attack the hill. They carried out a large-scale artillery bombardment of the German trenches and asked the 30th Engineers to follow up with a chemical attack to hinder rescue-and-repair efforts.[119]

Battle, 1918 49

On August 5 at 11 p.m., after extensive preparations, the gas soldiers launched three hundred mortar bombs and fired five hundred Livens projectors at German targets. One of the projector emplacements initially failed to launch, but a brave trio consisting of a sergeant, a private, and a farrier set out under enemy fire to repair the projectors and launch the gas. Two of the three were accidentally gassed during the exploit, and all were recommended for the Distinguished Service Cross.[120] The gas attack was credited with causing heavy enemy casualties. Subsequent intelligence gathered by the French indicated that the gas had caught the Germans unprepared and had resulted in an estimated eighty to one hundred deaths. The CWS was proud of this attack, later touting it as a "striking instance of the power of offensive-gas warfare when skillfully conducted."[121]

On August 9, the 30th Engineers were officially incorporated into the new CWS organization and renamed the 1st Gas Regiment.[122] Now under their more appropriate moniker, the gas soldiers went on to execute another large chemical attack. The 1st Gas was ordered to launch eight hundred Livens projectors near the town of Baccarat. This operation required ninety tons of chemical munitions, which the members of the regiment moved by rail car, truck, and burro to the projector emplacements in no-man's-land. In spite of the difficult logistics, the work was completed quickly because the area received almost no enemy artillery fire while the soldiers installed the projectors. The 1st Gas Regiment's chaplain, Addison, recorded that their billets far to the rear were under almost constant enemy bombardment, ironically "making rest more risky than work."[123] At midnight on August 17, the gas was launched with success. Slowly but surely, the army's chemical warfare soldiers felt they were demonstrating their effectiveness and earning trust and respect.

The AEF as a whole was still prone to suffer high numbers of casualties in German gas attacks, particularly when mustard gas was used. German artillery inundated the U.S. 89th Division with mustard gas the night of August 7 in the woods southeast of Seicheprey, causing 759 gas injuries and at least forty-seven deaths. Captain Edward Mack of the CWS understated the case when he wrote that "this was an inexcusably high number." "Some of the men," he said, "did not wear respirators at all, thinking that mustard gas was not dangerous. Others used the mouth-piece but did not protect their eyes by wearing the face-piece. Throughout the area about 75% of the men wore their respirators from 5 to 6 hours, but were gassed in the morning when they had to remove their respirators from exhaustion."[124]

A principal reason for the large number of casualties was that the soldiers were left in position even though the ground and trees around them had become saturated with mustard gas. A CWS report prepared after this tragedy admonished, "It is impossible to stand up under mustard gas. The only method of defense is withdrawal."[125] Yet often during a battle, or in its aftermath, withdrawal was inexpedient or impossible. Months later, during the Meuse-Argonne offensive, the 89th Division was bombarded by mustard gas while occupying another forest. The salient they defended was too strategically important to be abandoned, and even the division gas officer agreed that "it was worth 400 gas casualties not to have to evacuate the position that was won with such difficulty."[126] Mustard-gas casualties were the inevitable result of such decisions for the AEF.

In September the U.S. Army began its most ambitious offensive yet, at Saint-Mihiel. Involving more than half a million American troops, the objective was to defeat the German army in its defensive position around the city and force it to retreat eastward.[127] Saint-Mihiel was south of the besieged French city of Verdun, and pushing the German forces back from it was deemed an important and difficult task. At the outset of the Saint-Mihiel offensive, the 1st Gas Regiment was separated into small platoons and assigned to different individual army divisions to make it more responsive and versatile. The various platoons were ordered to participate in the opening assault by creating smoke screens and attacking German defenders with explosives and poisonous gasses. After that, they were expected to deploy smoke, gas, and explosives as required by their assigned divisions.[128]

The weather was abysmal in the days that led up to the offensive. It rained constantly; the muddy, traffic-congested roads were almost impassable. In spite of the added difficulty, the 1st Gas Regiment was ready with its equipment by the start of the offensive. On September 12 at the appointed hour, the AEF began a massive artillery assault across the entire theater of operations, and soldiers began their advance toward the German positions. Those first hours of the attack were full of "brilliance and excitement" for the soldiers of the gas regiment.[129] The gas platoons, scattered across the front, fired scores of weapons loaded with smoke bombs, poisonous gas, and incendiary and explosive liquids at their German targets in concert with the other elements of the 1st Army. The opening hours of the offensive were very successful, and the Germans began to fall back.

Afterward, however, the 1st Gas Regiment's participation in the offensive came to an unexpected end. The Germans were retreating too rapidly for the fighting front to stabilize, and the AEF's forward momentum made division commanders doubt the necessity and practicality of any more chemical attacks.[130] The AEF was also experiencing very few enemy chemical attacks during the fighting, and they did not want to invite retaliation by making more extensive use of poison gas.[131] By the end of the offensive on September 15, the 1st Gas Regiment had not made any more substantive contributions to the battle.

This turn of events was disappointing for the gas soldiers, who had wanted to play a much more active role in the fighting than they ultimately did. Addison wrote in his *Story of the 1st Gas Regiment* that his unit's participation in the Saint-Mihiel offensive should not be rated by its "actual value" but rather by its "potential value, the reckoning of what we might have done and should have done had occasion offered."[132] It is a story, he said, "of strain and effort, filled with carrying and reconnoitering, with watching and waiting."[133] Certainly, Addison and the other soldiers of the 1st Gas Regiment would rather have told a story about their participation in the battle that highlighted "actual value" over "potential value."

The last major offensive of World War I was the Meuse-Argonne offensive. It was the largest American campaign of the war, involving more than 1.2 million U.S. troops. The offensive lasted from September 1918 until the war ended and was fought in the Meuse River valley and the Argonne Forest. It was extremely difficult fighting. The Germans were stalwart defenders, and Americans described some of the skirmishes there as hell on earth.

> Upon the fields, along every approach, and in the trenches, still lay the dead. The whole country had been drenched with gas. Although the fields were sodden and every road-ditch was a running stream of water, the odor of charred things was everywhere as if the earth were still smoldering. One felt that all about him the hot breath of an unseen, evil power was fuming; and was glad for once that the rain was falling to destroy the hot poison in the air. . . . Amid universal desolation one felt as if he were treading haunted ground.[134]

Gas played an important role in the fighting for the German defenders, who seemed to appreciate that this might be their last chance to beat back the American and French advance. Most of the combat took place in wooded areas, which are particularly suited to gas attacks because the branches and leaf canopy act to close in the space and shelter the area from winds that would blow the poison air away. This made life on the front lines extremely difficult and dangerous for the soldiers. In one instance the 33rd Division was caught in a wooded area for several days, unable to advance. They were gassed constantly, and the absence of wind allowed the chemical clouds to remain persistent for long periods. Gas casualties were constantly being shuttled to rear-area hospitals, so much so that one division medical officer commented that "every officer and man in the Division, working with combat battalions and in other organizations operating . . . near the front, was gassed to some degree during the operations."[135] As bloody and noxious as the campaign was, the fighting in the Argonne resulted in the liberation of the French city of Sedan, which was a significant accomplishment. Sedan had been in German possession since the start of the war, and its railroads supported the German army throughout Northern France. The capture of the city brought World War I closer to an end, but at a high cost. The fighting resulted in approximately 117,000 U.S. casualties.[136]

At the beginning of the Meuse-Argonne offensive, the 1st Gas Regiment launched sixteen separate attacks along the American front lines, firing smoke, incendiary liquid, and explosives at the Germans, but no poisonous gas. After their initial participation, events followed what was by that time a familiar pattern. The regiment was ordered to keep pace with the U.S. advance and to assist as needed, but over the weeks of fighting, they seldom participated in offensive actions.[137] October 2 marked their first gas attack of the campaign, when a mere fifty-six Livens projectors were fired on German soldiers in the city of Vilosnes.[138] During the final weeks of World War I, the members of the 1st Gas Regiment conducted several mortar attacks and generated smoke screens, but orders to deploy chemical weapons remained infrequent.

Advancing against the Germans in Belgium, the 37th Division suffered sporadic gas shelling from October 31 to November 4. The Division Gas Officer, Captain I. W. Nowry, wrote a report about the attacks for the CWS, noting that the gas had managed to cause only thirty-one injuries and one death. The shelling was very unusual.

> In the opinion of the Division Gas Officer, the Germans were experiencing a shortage of gas shells in that Sector, as the attack lacked the systematic thoroughness which was usually characteristic of the German Gas shelling. Many times Mustard, D.A., and Phosgene were used at the same time and frequently one or all of these gasses were mixed with High Explosive shelling. The terrain affected was not at all favorable for a gas attack of any magnitude.[139]

The attacks had the characteristics of a disorganized rear-guard action. One week later Germany agreed to the armistice that ended hostilities. From the start of the Meuse-Argonne offensive to the November 11 armistice, the gas regiment conducted eighty-four individual operations, and only a handful of those had involved the use of poison gas. Those last few weeks constituted the bulk of the 1st Gas Regiments' combat activity, having only performed 133 individual combat actions over the course of the entire war.[140]

The 1st Gas Regiment's record of achievement, as such, is surely one that needs to be qualified. Their battlefield activities were usually limited to firing smoke and explosive weapons at the Germans in the opening hours of a battle, followed by long periods of relative inactivity. The bulk of the chemical weapons used against Germany during World War I were fired from American artillery units, and not from the CWS's Livens projectors. While the soldiers of the 1st Gas Regiment no doubt made a contribution to the fighting, it could not be said, as it would later be claimed by officers of the CWS, that chemical weapons had been key to winning the war. There was considerable speculation about the role that gas, and by extension the CWS, would have played on the battlefield had the war not ended when it did. One CWS officer who wrote about this potential in the postwar period was Augustin M. Prentiss: "All in all, it is clear from the plans of both sides that, had the war continued for another year, the campaign of 1919 would have been largely a chemical war. This phenomenal rise of chemicals from an unknown obscurity in 1915 to the position of a military agent of the first magnitude in 1918 is without parallel in the history of warfare."[141]

Another year of war, the CWS speculated, would have given the AEF another year to improve their defensive capabilities and perhaps to design and manufacture improved gas masks. The factories at Edgewood Arsenal could have been completed and brought to full production, and researchers might have innovated new poison gasses and delivery systems. While it was true that a lengthier war would have given the CWS more time to improve aspects of the U.S. chemical warfare program, there were no guarantees. An additional year of fighting would probably not have changed the opinions of regular army officers who avoided using gas because they viewed it as a dangerous and distasteful weapon. Gas soldiers who believed that 1919 had the potential to evolve into a "chemical war" relied on several suppositions that could not be proved, but the counterfactual was supported by several technological achievements the CWS had managed before the November armistice.

The members of the CWS were pioneers in the use of smoke-generating phosphorous. They had worked to perfect methods of creating smoke screens that could mask troop movements from ground and aerial observation, as well as create the illusion of army activity in areas where there was none. The CWS had also experimented with methods of concealing

Livens projector flashes (to prevent the enemy from being alerted to an imminent gas attack) and had created decoy flashes that they hoped would force the Germans to don their gas masks unnecessarily.[142] While directing CWS operations in France, Amos A. Fries proposed that airplanes be used to drop gas bombs on enemy cities.[143] The AEF's commander John J. Pershing refused the suggestion and established a policy that the U.S. Army would not intentionally gas civilians unless the Germans did so first, but forward-thinking CWS officers believed that airplanes had the potential to deliver chemical weapons to enemy targets in the future. Before the First World War ended, CWS soldiers also experimented with using a liquid incendiary called thermite as a weapon. "Like a great many other promising things in war, it didn't entirely prove out," Fries wrote of thermite. "Nevertheless," he said, "it was sufficiently successful as manufactured by the British and as used by the Americans to give it a place in past history and a probable place in future military operations."[144]

The most promising technological innovation the CWS achieved during World War I was the manufacture of a new, lethal war gas that was developed too late to be used by the AEF. Working at the CWS laboratory at Catholic University in Washington, D.C., Captain Winford Lee Lewis developed a substance that had been discovered in the United States in 1904 by a priest-chemist, Father Julius Arthur Nieuwland. Made by combining arsenic tetrachloride and acetylene, the black liquid produced an odor that hospitalized Nieuwland for several days. Nieuwland abandoned work on the compound because he saw no practical use for something so poisonous, but he mentioned it briefly in his innocuously titled PhD thesis, "Some Reactions of Acetylene." Lewis heard about the experiment from a professor at Catholic University who had been Nieuwland's advisor, Father John Griffin, and once he took up the research the substance came to be called Lewisite. Lewis delivered the formula to James B. Conant, who designed and constructed a Lewisite factory in Willoughby, Ohio, with his associate Frank M. Dorsey.[145]

Lewisite was an extremely exciting development in chemical-weapons research for the CWS. Researchers likened the substance to a more powerful mustard gas and, because so few people were aware of its existence, the mass production of Lewisite could be accomplished in secrecy. After only a few months of fighting alongside its more experienced allies, the AEF was going to employ Lewisite to surprise the Germans on the Western Front with a new, American-made war gas. It was anticipated that the Lewisite manufactured at Willoughby would be used in the 1919 spring offensive, but, of course, that event never materialized. The war ended before any Lewisite could be shipped across the Atlantic, and the CWS quietly disposed of the factory equipment and stockpiled chemicals.[146] It was not until confirmed rumors about Lewisite and the factory at Willoughby appeared in the press later in 1919 that the CWS abandoned secrecy and permitted its officers to boast about the achievement.[147]

Throughout 1918, as the CWS worked to train the AEF, manufacture chemical weapons, and use poison gas on the battlefield, gas soldiers argued that their method of war represented the most substantive military achievement of the First World War. "Gas warfare is not a fad, nor an experiment," CWS director William L. Sibert asserted. "It is a proven, powerful instrument of war both in offense and defense."[148] However, there was little basis for such claims.[149] CWS suppositions about the important role chemical weapons had played in the war were belied by the relatively limited use of gas made on the battlefield. While no one knew what potential gas might have as a weapon in future wars, its detractors considered the past prologue.

3 Crisis, 1919–1920

The future of the Chemical Warfare Service (CWS) and chemical weapons was uncertain in the postwar world. In 1919 the American public reacted against modern weapons in general and poison gas in particular because of the battlefield suffering it had caused. Policymakers in the Department of War and the U.S. Army had formed negative impressions of chemical weapons during World War I, and they attempted to limit all chemical warfare activities in the armed forces after the armistice. Faced with the likely elimination of their area of service, the officers of the CWS, principally under the leadership of Amos A. Fries, organized to oppose anti-gas sentiment and promote chemical weapons. The CWS fought a public-relations campaign and ultimately convinced Congress to allow the organization to remain intact within the Department of War. During this fight over chemical warfare policy in the U.S. military, the CWS also managed to lay a foundation that would allow them to continue improve their reputation through the 1920s.

The U.S. government moved to reduce defense spending drastically once the war had ended. Expenditures for the Department of War in 1919 totaled almost 9 billion dollars, because Congress had already approved the budget for that year with the expectation that the First World War would still be unresolved. The following year, however, that amount was lowered to 1 billion dollars. In 1921 expenditures were further reduced to 463 million, and by 1925 they had sunk to 252 million.[1] Shrinking military expenditures sharply reduced the personnel strength of the CWS. After the end of World War I the number of personnel authorized for the CWS was reduced from a wartime level of 600 officers and 3,000 enlisted men, to 124 officers and 1,348 enlisted men.² Their extremely lean budget kept the CWS from reaching its authorized strength throughout the 1920s. In 1922, for example, the CWS reported having only 87 officers and 550 enlisted men.³

However, the postwar budgetary concerns of the CWS were overshadowed by a rising anti-gas sentiment. The public considered gas far more heinous than the artillery shells, machine guns, tanks, and battleships that were used during World War I. One reason for this aversion: gas is literally "poison," a method of killing that has been condemned for centuries as treacherous and cowardly.⁴ During the First World War, Americans temporarily set aside their objections to chemical weapons and tacitly approved of the use of poison gas by the American Expeditionary Force (AEF) because other warring powers were already using it; once the war ended, however, public antipathy for poison gas returned in strength.⁵

The relatively large numbers of gas casualties that the AEF had suffered helped secure chemical warfare's reputation for having been one of the most terrible aspects of World War I. The U.S. Army Surgeon General reported that the AEF sustained more than seventy thousand poison-gas casualties in the war—nearly 30 percent of the total U.S. casualties in the war and a higher percentage of chemical warfare casualties than any other nation's army.⁶ Poison gas was also a weapon that was associated with America's German enemies. Germany had been the first nation to use poison gas effectively during the war, and that fact had been prominently featured in American propaganda. In a speech he gave at a patriotic event in Portsmouth, Ohio, on June 20, 1918, Governor James M. Cox said, "Germany violated her solemn compact with other nations never to use poisonous gas in warfare," adding that "the shame of that nation will not soon be forgotten."⁷ People who believed that Germany's use of poison gas constituted a criminal act began to discuss ending the future use of chemical weapons. Similar attitudes prevailed in countries outside the United States. In Great Britain, Cambridge University geneticist and poison-gas enthusiast John Burdon Sanderson Haldane wrote of chemical warfare: "The public mind has to a large extent reacted against the opinions impressed on it during the war by official propaganda."⁸ Negative opinions about chemical weapons predominated in Germany as well. Fritz Haber, a leading scientist in the German gas program during the war, believed that condemnations of chemical warfare were illogical, and in the postwar years he repeatedly defended the use of poison-gas weapons.⁹

Peace, labor, civic, women's, and religious groups, many of whom experienced a revival between the world wars, attacked poison gas as a principal example of the evils of war almost immediately after World

War I ended.[10] Journalist and peace author Will Irwin used chemical weapons as evidence of the inhumanity of war in his widely read book, *The Next War: An Appeal to Common Sense*.[11] Religious figures such as Harry Emerson Fosdick, one of America's most celebrated preachers, echoed this sentiment. From his pulpit at the First Presbyterian Church of New York City on June 5, 1921, Fosdick delivered his famous sermon "Shall We End War?" in which he argued that weapons were becoming too dangerous to humanity ever to be used safely again. Now that chemical weapons had been used in war, Fosdick said, "there is no man living with imagination adequate to picture what war is going to be."[12] The advent of mustard gas, tanks, airplanes, and other weapons of World War I also led fiction writers in the postwar decades to begin emphasizing in war novels and short stories the dangers of war and the destructive power of modern armaments.[13] The changes in the way that authors portrayed war reflected the public's changed perception of warfare.

Worse yet for the CWS, the use of poisonous and suffocating gasses was seen by many members of the military as a method of warfare that did not befit a soldier. U.S. Army Chief of Staff Peyton C. March was one of the most prominent opponents of the CWS after the First World War. During the postwar period he tried to abolish the CWS entirely. In his memoirs March acknowledged arguments that chemical weapons could be important for future national defense, but, he wrote, "The use of poison gas carried wherever the wind listeth, kills the birds of the air, and may kill women and children in the rear of the firing line."[14] During the war March visited army hospitals that treated gas casualties in the aftermath of attacks, and he wrote that "the sufferings of . . . children, particularly, were horrible and produced a profound impression on me."[15] He called gas warfare "cruel," "savage," "repugnant," "barbarous," and he asserted that if the United States continued to work with such weapons, it "had much to answer for."[16]

The CWS also faced some opposition from General John J. Pershing, former commander of the AEF and the most respected soldier of his generation. The CWS tended to count Pershing as a chemical warfare supporter because he occasionally made public statements about the need to continue poison-gas work. In his well-known and widely quoted *Final Report*, Pershing wrote that "whether or not gas will be employed in future wars is a matter of conjecture, but the effect is so deadly to the unprepared that we can never afford to neglect the question."[17] Pershing spoke favorably of the army chemical warfare program on several other occasions, the most important of which was before a joint House and Senate committee hearing on army reorganization on November 1,

1919.[18] His statements there were generally curt, though, and his testimony focused on other aspects of the postwar military to a far greater extent. Later, during the Washington Conference on the Limitation of Armaments in 1921, Pershing withdrew his supposed support for the CWS and worked to end chemical warfare by international agreement.

Many more junior officers throughout the U.S. military also opposed the continuation of the CWS after World War I.[19] Some proposed making the CWS part of the Ordnance Department or the Corps of Engineers in lieu of ending the chemical warfare program outright. The members of the CWS resisted incorporation into other departments and defended their organization's independence. "I am firmly of the opinion that if the chemical work of the Army is put under the Corps of Engineers it will rapidly run down and its development will finally cease altogether," the wartime commander of Edgewood Arsenal, William H. Walker, wrote. "If the Chemical Warfare Service is placed into an environment which, while not hostile to it, has no interest in it," he said, "[then] it will be shoved out of the current of affairs and will naturally stagnate."[20] Amos A. Fries agreed that loss of the organization's autonomy would lead to institutional degradation, writing, "As a part of another organization whose experience and precedents for a half century are along totally different lines it could not get anything except secondary consideration, and if it kept distinct in another Service such as the Ordnance Department there could result only confusion, dissension and enormously decreased efficiency. All pride of profession would be lost, and with it the success of the Service."[21]

Amos Alfred Fries was the CWS officer who led the effort to protect the independence and integrity of the army's chemical warfare organization during the postwar period. Fries was born in Wisconsin on March 17, 1873, but spent his childhood on his parent's farm in Missouri and moved with them to Eugene, Oregon just before finishing high school. After graduating he briefly became a teacher before securing a commission to West Point from Congressmen Binger Herman in 1894. Going to West Point and joining the army was purportedly something that Fries had expressed an interest in since he was young. He graduated high in his class in 1898 and was commissioned an officer in the Corps of Engineers. He and his classmates all matriculated from West Point a few weeks early that year for them to be able to fight in the Spanish American War, which had been declared that April.[22]

Fries spent the war across the Pacific Ocean building roads, bridges, and other construction to help the army fight insurgency in the Philippines. After that, he traveled back to the United States to build infrastructure for the National Park Service and work on harbor projects along the West Coast. From 1911 to 1914 Fries served as director of military engineering at the Army Engineering School in Washington, D.C. He served there for a time as editor of the official publication of the Corps of Engineers, an experience that served him later in the CWS, where he established a weekly journal to support the continuation of chemical weapons work in the United States after the war.[23]

When World War I was declared, Fries was building roads in Yellowstone National Forest. He was sent to France and briefly served as director of roads before being ordered to lead the embryonic Gas Service. "I had been in France five days," Fries recalled, "when I was informed—I think on the night of the 17th or 18th of August—that I probably would be named chief of the gas service."[24] Though the assignment came as a surprise to him, Fries served as gas chief for the war's duration, organizing and coordinating U.S. chemical warfare operations in France. Fries became a tireless gas enthusiast and consistently worked to expand the role of the CWS during World War I. For his service Fries received the French Legion of Honor, the British Companion of St. Michael and St. George, and the American Distinguished Service Medal.[25]

Fries was stationed at Edgewood Arsenal, Maryland, after the armistice, and was ordered to serve under the Director of the CWS, William L. Sibert. In September 1919, Fries visited the scene of an accidental explosion at an Edgewood Arsenal warehouse, where he was inadvertently gassed by the poisons released at the site. Fries suffered no permanent injury but experienced dizziness and exhaustion for days after the exposure. "After this experience," Fries wrote afterward, "believe me, I shall look out the next time."[26] Though he had personally experienced gas poisoning, Fries spent the postwar years trying to improve people's perceptions of chemical weapons. The long-term security of the CWS depended on encouraging an appreciation for poison gas among military policymakers.

From Fries's perspective, the rest of the U.S. Army began behaving as if the end of World War I meant the end of chemical warfare once the armistice was reached. The armistice agreement with Germany required its military to turn weapon stockpiles over to the United States and the other Allies, to become part of their arsenal or to be sold as scrap. The soldiers of the AEF discarded poison gas seized from the Germans instead of keeping or repurposing it. One contemporary chemist wrote of this practice that "the idea prevails that chemical munitions should be destroyed because they were designed for a purpose which has ceased to exist." "It would be just as reasonable," he continued, "to throw the steel and other materials designed for use as shells into Chesapeake Bay because they will not be needed for war purposes."[27] The fact that chemical weapons were being destroyed and other munitions were not sent a message that "now that the war is over, we do not need chemists or chemistry anymore."[28]

German gas was not the only relic of chemical warfare being discarded. U.S. soldiers turning in their equipment before their voyage back home were reporting their gas masks "lost" in significant numbers. Now that they were no longer threatened by gas attacks, some of the doughboys were simply ditching the masks across the French countryside. J. Allan Sampson, a captain in the 2nd Army at the Thauvenot Barracks, complained after the armistice, "I can certify that the road between here and the quay where the men entertain, and more especially the quay itself, is covered, either with the entire masks or with the box and face mask, the men using the case as a musette bag."[29] It seemed to the CWS at the end of World War I that the entire army, from officers to enlisted men, treated the end of gas warfare as a foregone conclusion. The prevailing attitude was that the immediate end of hostilities represented the end of gas warfare forever.

If that presumption about the end of chemical warfare were correct, it followed that there would be no further need for the CWS either. In the postwar demobilization, most of the gas soldiers were either discharged or reassigned to unrelated positions as engineers or instructors, and many were officers who had served with Fries personally. Colonel J. W. N. Schultz, for example, was assigned to the army school at Leavenworth to be an engineering and chemical warfare instructor, although he told Fries he was asked to "go easy" on chemical warfare.[30] The commander of the 1st Gas Regiment, Earl J. Atkisson, was for a time reassigned to teach engineering at the army infantry school at Ft. Benning, Georgia. Fries called this transfer "the limit of absurdity."[31] Fries himself was nearly assigned to the Army Corps of Engineers in New Orleans, Louisiana, once the war ended. After an intercession with the Army Personnel Section, Fries managed to halt his transfer and remain in the CWS. Fries believed that Army Chief of Staff March was working with Chief of Engineers William M. Black to "destroy the Chemical Warfare Service" through these transfers.[32]

The abolition of the CWS seemed inevitable until Fries arrived back in the United States and successfully stalled the process. Fries asked for help from two members of Congress, Senator George E. Chamberlain and Representative Julius Kahn. Fries had met Kahn on a trip to the Philippines before World War I, and Chamberlain had been governor of Oregon when Fries had done some river and harbor work there with the Corps of Engineers.[33] Fries implored them to continue the CWS temporarily, along with other new technical services like the Tank Corps and the Air Service, until any final decisions could be made about how the postwar army should be structured. Kahn and Chamberlain, who were on the House and Senate military committees, respectively, agreed. They helped secure speedy passage of the 1st Army Reorganization Bill on July 11, 1919, which continued the current wartime organization of the army through June 30, 1920. Fries said that getting the legislation passed by Congress "was a very hard fight, in fact, so hard that it was not until the very last moment that we were sure we were not going out of business."[34] However, the law represented only a temporary victory. Fries and the CWS now had just one year to convince Congress to keep them in business permanently.

To accomplish this, Fries relied on a network of like-minded colleagues whose positions, skills, or associations could be useful to the embattled service. Many of the men involved were former officers of the CWS who had been discharged at the end of the First World War. Naturally, officers who were released from the CWS generally secured employment in the civilian chemical industry or in universities. The CWS aided and encouraged this process. The industrial relations section of the service provided job placement assistance at the end of the war for outgoing officers. When hiring "executives, engineers, superintendents, plant operators, foremen, supervisors and salesmen," said an article published by the CWS in the industry periodical *Chemical and Metallurgical Engineering*, "preference should be shown those who have served their country in the war."[35] "Kindly employ and recommend them when opportunity occurs," the article asked, and it invited any chemical firm with positions available to phone the Service directly with their needs.

Fries conducted an extensive correspondence with these former officers in 1919 and 1920. On one occasion, Fries had a list of discharged officers with their present occupations and mailing addresses compiled.[36] He kept peers updated on events that affected the CWS, sent them copies of his notes and articles, and wrote to them with suggestions about what they could do to aid his efforts; they often sent Fries suggestions as well. Such was the case when Colonel E. N. Johnston, an officer stationed at the Lakehurst proving grounds, wrote to Fries in September 1919. "Captain Hudson C. Millar, C.W.S., who has just been demobilized," Johnston wrote, "has known quite well Senator Simmons, Senator Overman and Representative Nichols of South Carolina, a member of the House Military Committee. He has offered to write these gentlemen in the interest of the propaganda work which you are now doing."[37] Fries wrote a reply to Johnston a few days later:

> I shall send Captain Millar a lot of data from which he can take that which appeals to him and which he thinks will appeal to Senators and

Congressmen whom he mentioned. In that connection I just yesterday talked with Captain W. B. Anderson, Secretary to the Military Affairs Committee of the House, and he told me that you had at Lakehurst with you, he thought, two officers by the name of Ferrett and McBride. He mentioned that he thinks these are most excellent men for the Service in that they know a lot of men around Congress.[38]

Fries created a network of informed supporters through his correspondence. He educated them about chemical warfare, kept them updated on the status of legislation in Congress, and urged them to contact members of the House and the Senate in support of the CWS. One typical letter written by Fries began with the words "inclosed herewith are some ideas that I think need the attention of all technical societies, journals, and individuals in the U.S. If you agree with me, get busy and spread the gospel."[39] Fries aimed to get as many technical societies, journals, and individuals as he could to spread the word.

In September 1919 Fries gathered a small group of former CWS officers to organize and finance a publicity campaign that would attempt to gain the attention of the American public and convince them that the CWS should continue its work. He believed a robust public relations campaign was the only way to ensure the service's survival. "As is proper in republican form of government, sooner or later our cause must stand or fall on the appeal it makes to the average man," Fries wrote. "Our proposition is absolutely sound and I have the utmost faith that if we can get it properly before the public it cannot be beaten by any group of men."[40]

The group Fries formed included William H. Chadbourne, a former CWS major, who organized veterans of the CWS into the Chemical Warfare Service Association to lobby Congressmen to support the service, and Charles E. Richardson, another former CWS major, who was employed by the International Coal Products Corporation in New York. Richardson used his connections in the chemical industry to publicize the CWS, and Fries described him as "the militant driving force" of the effort.[41] A former lieutenant colonel named Richmond Mayo-Smith, who became a publisher in Massachusetts after the war, was Fries's "cool manager, weighing every turn and crook of the game."[42] Fries and these others attempted to influence public policy by appealing to as many members of the American public as possible.

To help promote the CWS, Fries authorized the creation of a weekly periodical named *Chemical Warfare*. It was ostensibly a newsletter for the personnel of Edgewood Arsenal, but *Chemical Warfare*'s editors hoped that the paper "would prove an agent of publicity, not only for Edgewood Arsenal, but for the Chemical Warfare Service as a whole."[43] According to the first issue, published on August 21, 1919, the paper was intended to be read by military and civilian personnel, as well as "friends and former associates who since have re-entered pursuits in civil life."[44] *Chemical Warfare* was designed to advertise the accomplishments of the CWS to the same groups of people Fries was trying to reach through his extensive person-to-person correspondence.

The outlook of *Chemical Warfare* can be inferred from this list of twenty-five possible masthead slogans that were submitted to Fries for approval.

1. GAS killed the GERM in GERMANY
2. GAS is war's WORST enemy
3. GAS—The new dictator of peace
4. GAS—The army's new right hand
5. The "C.W.S."—Watch it grow!
6. GAS puts a new PUNCH in the FIST of Uncle Sam
7. GAS warfare—A policeman's club for world peace
8. EDGEWOOD KNOWS HOW!
9. The "C.W.S."—A powerful factor in war—Will prove the same in peace
10. EDGEWOOD MADE GOOD!
11. A well-developed "C.W.S." means peace protection.
12. Gas warfare—The military arm of the future.
13. The "C.W.S." GASSED the GERM in GERMANY
14. GAS WINS!
15. EDGEWOOD HAS A FUTURE
16. Gas warfare—The League of Nations' policeman
17. BOOST EDGEWOOD!
18. COOPERATION SPELLS SUCCESS
19. The RIGHT spirit of cooperation paves the way for PROGRESS and SUCCESS
20. The service with the right kind of spirit WINS
21. The "C.W.S." is the service with a future
22. A heavy concentration of gas warfare development may keep the COVER on that peace PRESERVE JAR
23. Chemical Warfare Service—A brand new branch of service which offers a FUTURE with real OPPORTUNITIES
24. E dgewood Arsenal
    D oes things—
    G ets results:
    E nergetic
    W ork
    O ffers
    O pportunities for
    D evelopment

25. G as is the
A rmy's new
S econd ace[45]

The CWS was advertised as a novel organization that made important contributions to the war effort. The slogans implied that the CWS was full of potential and vigor and that it would work to aid the nation and preserve international peace after the war.

Articles written by Fries frequently appeared in *Chemical Warfare*. Some were informative commentaries about gas warfare, others were about the importance of chemists and the CWS to national defense. Fries penned a stirring call to arms for the inaugural issue:

> Just as no man is ever whipped until he quits fighting, so no cause is ever lost until its friends give up the struggle. We, in the Chemical Warfare Service, have a hard battle ahead of us, but the cause is right and just and will make for the future greatness of our country, and every true American, man or woman, should be proud to engage in a fight when right and justice is on his side.[46]

The most original and significant articles Fries composed were about what he termed "the humanity" of chemical warfare. In October 1919 *Chemical Warfare* published a lengthy exposition of this thesis, "The Humanity of Poison Gas."[47] In that article, and in others like it, Fries countered the arguments made by CWS critics who believed that chemical weapons were barbaric. "There is a popular notion that gas warfare is the most horrible method of warfare ever invented, and that it will be abolished because it is so horrible," Fries wrote. "And yet it is not horrible."[48] He articulated a pro-gas position, based on the assertion that the effects of poison gasses on the body were far less grotesque and traumatic than the wounds caused by bullets, artillery shells, and explosives. Fries cited statistical proof: "The measure of humanity for any form of warfare is the percentage of deaths to the total number injured by the particular method of warfare under consideration."[49] This was his gauge, because the casualty statistics available from the war indicated that a very low percentage of soldiers who were exposed to gas died from the exposure; specifically, the U.S. Army Surgeon General's Office calculated that out of 70,552 soldiers who were gassed in the American Expeditionary Force, only 1,221 (less than 2 percent) of them died as a result.[50] Fries and others in the CWS asserted throughout the 1920s that chemical warfare was, therefore, the most ideal and humane form of war in modern history. Casualty data made poison gas appear to be a weapon that would incapacitate, rather than kill, and would allow the majority of soldiers to eventually recover and return to their homes and families.

The statistics from the Surgeon General's Office that the CWS used are the best available, but the data is problematic. The information was gathered from U.S. field hospitals scattered across France during the war.[51] Errors could naturally have occurred, given that during World War I, physicians in uniform who had never encountered a chemical warfare patient before 1918 had to decide if a soldier had been gassed or merely suffered from a cough or conjunctivitis. Soldiers were sometimes known to fake an injury or self-inflict a wound to avoid combat duty, and military doctors were responsible for identifying the malingerers. That was a difficult enough task when it came to discernable lacerations or broken bones, but it was much more difficult when soldiers who complained of difficulty breathing had no other observable symptoms. Some chemicals, like mustard gas, even had a delayed physiological effect wherein symptoms would not appear until hours after exposure. A soldier who had been gassed might not receive the benefit of the doubt from a careless or overworked doctor, and he could be returned to service without being recorded as a casualty or being treated.[52]

Moreover, no accurate reckoning can be made of the number of soldiers who died of gas poisoning outside of a field hospital. Cause of death cannot always be determined for soldiers killed outright on the battlefield; accordingly, the percentage of those deaths caused by chemical weapons will never be known. Likewise, gassed soldiers who were missing in action, captured by the enemy, treated at a British or French hospital, or who appeared to have superficial wounds treated at the front lines, would not have visited a U.S. hospital and could not be recorded as gas casualties.

In fact, there was evidence that the percentage of poison gas combat deaths was much higher. From April to December 1917, the British Army compiled data from interviews with German prisoners of war about the casualties caused by chemical weapons. Fries had an abridged version of the report prepared for him in 1918. The statistics gathered by the British indicated that a substantial number of German soldiers exposed to chemical weapons in battle were killed. In some cases 25 percent or more of German chemical warfare casualties died from the exposure.[53]

Assuming that the numbers gathered by the U.S. Surgeon General's Office were completely accurate, they were still not necessarily a measure of the humanity of chemical weapons. The statistics could also be regarded as a measure of the weapons' ineffectiveness. Non-lethal chemical agents used in World War I, such as sneezing agents and tear gasses, were designed to harass and incapacitate. Lethal alternatives such as phosgene and mustard gas were not developed to make the fighting more humane. The claims made by chemical warfare proponents about the humanity of poison gas were belied by the lethality that was intended.

Most important, veterans who had been gassed in combat knew all too well that humanity is not something that can be easily quantified. Hearing poison gas called "humane" in 1922, U.S. Army veteran A. Reid Moir wrote, "Is it humane to lie in excruciating pain, with stomach swollen by the expansion of gas, and with lungs eaten by the deadly vapor to cough up one's life in an agonizing convulsion? This, sir, may not sound very beautiful, but it is far less beautiful to see . . . gas is not only 'inhumane'; it is not far from 'hellish.'"[54] Despite the lasting psychological impression that gas left on veterans who had experienced it, Fries and other CWS officers zealously promoted the idea that chemical warfare was better and more humane than other forms of war throughout the 1920s.

In 1919, Edgewood Arsenal began to scale back its operations as the civilians who had worked there relocated, the temporary buildings were removed, and the remaining military personnel shut down the production facilities. The various poison-gas factories they had built were shuttered, and the equipment inside them greased and disconnected. Some of the chlorine gas stored at Edgewood was shipped to Panama to be used for water treatment, and some of the phosgene reserve was sold to glass-making companies for removing iron oxide from sand.[55] In the peacetime calm, the personnel barracks and other buildings on the grounds were given fresh coats of paint, and all the doors and window frames were painted the olive-green color "assumed by brass when exposed to chlorine fumes."[56] In July Fries ordered the installation of a weathervane on a chlorine tower, because "as the season advances and the gas containers get a little older we will probably have leaks somewhat oftener," so personnel downwind would need to be warned if they were in danger.[57] Fries prohibited Edgewood soldiers from wearing the insignia badges of their former areas of service on their uniforms, ordering them to wear the proper CWS insignia badge instead (composed of two crossed chemical flasks, called retorts).[58] As well, he proposed renaming Edgewood Arsenal "Hanlon Field," after the first gas officer killed in France, but the suggestion was not adopted.[59] All wartime construction projects ended, and Edgewood Arsenal was settling into an anticipated period of relative inactivity, but the CWS hoped to remain a permanent institution within the military and to maintain Edgewood until its facilities were needed again.

During the year between the passage of the 1st Army Reorganization Bill and what would be the 2nd in the summer of 1920, CWS officers at Edgewood worked with allies in the American chemical industry to convince Congress, and the nation, that their organization should continue chemical warfare work permanently. Professional chemists and the nation's major chemical producers actively supported the CWS throughout the postwar period. Concern about the fate of the CWS diffused into the private sector along with its personnel once the war ended, as many of its former officers found jobs as civilian chemists after their discharge, but the chemical industry had a strong relationship with the CWS even before that.

The U.S. chemical industry had been relatively nonexistent before World War I. It underwent a rapid expansion in 1917 and 1918 to accommodate the nation's need for weapons and other military supplies. The American dye industry was particularly important to the CWS, since many First World War–era chemical weapons were manufactured from byproducts of the commercial-dye manufacturing process. The overwhelming majority of dyes used in America were produced in Germany prior to the war, and finding domestic suppliers when they were needed was difficult. To aid in the rapid expansion of the U.S. dye industry, the federal government helped manufacturers to violate commercial law by seizing German patents and allowing their use. The lack of imported dyes on the market caused demand to exceed supply, and the U.S. industry began to grow considerably. The U.S. Department of Commerce calculated that the value of all nationally produced chemical dyes and extracts in 1914 was $20,620,336. By the end of the war in 1919, the value had increased to $53,744,283.[60]

Although many U.S. chemical manufacturers profited in wartime, by the end of the fighting most had not grown enough to be considered commercially competitive without substantial government support. Lacking protective tariffs to restrict chemical imports, and without the military purchasing their products, what was to become of the chemical industry now that the war was over? The industry as a whole believed it was in crisis, and its interests ran parallel to those of the CWS. The U.S. chemical industry and the CWS both found themselves at risk after World War I, and they worked in separate areas of the same field, so they supported each other through the 1920s.

The businessmen and scientists who worked with the CWS through the uncertain postwar period used several professional journals to spread information and ideas. They printed articles and editorials that promoted chemical manufacturing as it related to chemical weapons and the CWS.

When the Department of War announced that it was urging Congress to discontinue the CWS in August 1919, a mountain of opposition rose from these professional journals and the organizations that supported them. In an editorial titled "War Department Deserts Chemical Warfare Service," the journal *Chemical and Metallurgical Engineering* asserted, "It is true that the Chemical Warfare Service probably did not cut a fine military figure, but it brought to bear on the war a knowledge of things unknown to the Army and which will continue to be a closed book if the Service is abandoned as recommended." The editors concluded, "We have given this matter careful consideration, and it is with neither heat nor emotion that we express our opinion that the War Department is seriously in error in the plan about to be adopted."[61]

One month later the American Chemical Society held its annual meeting in Philadelphia. The army reorganization bill was a main topic of discussion. The society unanimously passed a resolution on behalf of its 13,500 members that protested the bill and supported the continuation of the CWS. They published the resolution and sent a copy to James W. Wadsworth Jr., the chairman of the Senate Committee on Military Affairs. "It has nothing to do with urging gas warfare upon military authorities," the society claimed, "but it does urge upon the Government the necessity of being prepared against it, and the only way to do this in regard to chemical problems is to have it done by chemists in a chemical division and under the supervision of chemists."[62] Another professional journal, *The Chemical Engineer*, published their support of the American Chemical Society resolution: "To approve of the resolution passed at the Philadelphia meeting of the Chemical Society protesting against the practical abolition of the Chemical Warfare Service seems such an obvious thing to do that it is difficult for one to conceive of the state of mind of one who holds a contrary opinion. Chemical warfare seems to have become . . . an essential part of the offensive and defensive military equipment of the armies of the world."[63] These public statements demonstrated the strength of support the CWS enjoyed within professional chemistry organizations.

Charles Holmes Herty's *Journal of Industrial and Engineering Chemistry* had perhaps the closest working relationship with the CWS through the 1920s. Born in Milledgeville, Georgia, in 1867, Herty earned his doctorate in chemistry from Johns Hopkins University in 1890, moving on to become a faculty member at the University of Georgia and a chemist at the U.S. Bureau of Forestry, where he developed an improved method of extracting turpentine from pine trees that helped revitalize the turpentine industry. Herty became one of the most prominent chemists in the country and frequently served as an expert policy advisor to various government agencies. He was president of the American Chemical Society and the Synthetic Organic Chemical Manufacturers Association, and from 1917 to 1921 he served as editor of the *Journal of Industrial and Engineering Chemistry*.

Herty used his personal and professional connections with chemists who entered government or military service to solicit information and articles for his journal. Beginning in February 1919, *Industrial and Engineering Chemistry* regularly featured contributions from the CWS published in a separate section of each issue. The section typically included two to four articles submitted by members of the CWS, written on such subjects as the wartime activities of the service or about new chemical and engineering processes being researched by army chemists. Herty's efforts on behalf of the CWS went beyond the print on the pages of his journal. After the First World War he went to work personally writing to and visiting colleagues, military officers, and congressmen, lobbying for the CWS to be maintained as a permanent part of the national defense establishment. In one letter, Herty asserted that to disband the CWS would be "a direct slam at the technical organizations of this country."[64] He testified before Congress at hearings surrounding the army reorganization bill, helped organize professional civilian chemists, and wrote editorials to newspapers across the country in support of the CWS during its struggle to remain a permanent organization.

As the members of the CWS worked to get chemists and other civilian professionals interested in chemical-weapons work, questions over secrecy and security began to arise. Relatively basic security measures had not been put in place at Edgewood Arsenal during World War I. In the summer of 1919 the CWS considered requiring standard identification for all civilian visitors and employees at the chemical-weapons plants there. Edgewood personnel badges were designed to be imprinted with the wearer's photo, thumbprint, and descriptive information.[65] One year later Fries considered requiring all personnel permanently stationed at Edgewood to swear an oath of secrecy.[66] Astonishingly, the CWS made a practice of sending samples of chemical weapons to any civilians who requested them by letter. The chemicals were made available in order to encourage researchers to experiment with poison gas, but in July 1919 the safety of the practice was questioned. "It is believed that a policy should be established for not giving out poisonous gasses for experimentation except to persons known to be absolutely reliable," Fries wrote in a memorandum.[67] He predicted that "sooner or later criminals are going to begin fooling with gasses," so he recommended to his superiors that a record be kept of all the people in the United States experimenting with war gasses and suggested that the record be coordinated with the Secret Service.[68]

The members of the CWS established these partnerships with civilian chemists in an attempt to influence members of Congress who were crafting the Army Reorganization Bill of 1920. To help persuade the legislative branch to allow the CWS to continue its work, Fries often directed his supporters to write or speak to members of Congress in favor of chemical warfare. In September 1919, for example, Fries wrote a letter to a former CWS colonel, Gilbert N. Lewis, who was at that time a member of the University of California's chemistry department. The letter began by discussing military awards but quickly turned to the army reorganization legislation. Fries thanked Lewis for sending a telegram on the subject to Representative Julius Kahn, chairman of the Committee on Military Affairs, and talked about how the bill was faring in Congress so far. Fries ended the letter, though, by asking for more help with Kahn and his family.

> Congressman Kahn's son Julius Kahn, Jr., is a student in the University of California and is taking the chemical course. Mrs. Kahn mentioned that she would be delighted to have her son become personally acquainted with you and Hildebrand [another former CWS officer now teaching at UC], of whom they have heard a great deal from me. She thinks it would add to Julius, Jr's ambition. I think also a little notice from you and Colonel Hildebrand might have a good effect on Mr. Kahn's attitude toward the Chemical Warfare Service.[69]

Personal favors, lunch engagements, letters and handshakes: these were the weapons that the CWS used in its campaign against Congress.

In August 1919 the U.S. Senate Subcommittee on Army Reorganization, of the Committee on Military Affairs, began a round of hearings about the bill. They solicited testimony from dozens of experts, inside and outside of the military. The CWS did not fare well at the outset of these hearings. The first expert called to give testimony was an ardent chemical warfare opponent, Army Chief of Staff Peyton C. March, who testified, bluntly, that "the War Department believes that the Chemical Warfare Service ought to be abolished," and he characterized chemical weapons as tools of war that were not suited to a civilized nation.[70] Senator George E. Chamberlain and Senator Charles S. Thomas, both supporters of the CWS, questioned March about how the Army would defend itself from an enemy who used poison gas. March replied that once the CWS was abolished, the Engineering Department of the army would take responsibility for designing and manufacturing defensive equipment like gas masks so that U.S. soldiers would remain safe.[71]

During his testimony, March brought up an accident that had occurred at American University as an example of how the continuation of chemical weapons research could put the public at risk. In August 1918 a cloud of poisonous gas was released from the CWS laboratory there, causing several injuries as it floated through the surrounding neighborhoods. The senators were familiar with this incident because a former member of that committee, Senator Nathan Bay Scott, was one of those seriously injured by the gas.[72]

March's testimony was followed at the hearing several days later by that of General Robert L. Bullard, who was one of the most prominent U.S. commanders of World War I. He testified that he hoped the army chemical warfare program would be continued, but when he was asked whether it should be part of the Engineering Department or be, instead, its own independent service, Bullard replied, "I do not care how or where it is put."[73] The next expert to testify, General James W. McAndrew, commandant of the Army General Staff College, said that he was in favor of the CWS, but "if we could by any agreement among the nations of the world do away with the use of poisonous gas in warfare, I am in favor of doing away with it."[74] Several days later Secretary of War Newton D. Baker testified that the chemical warfare duties of the army "ought to be in the Engineers."[75] He said that he hoped to make the Engineering Department the center of scientific activity in the U.S. military.

It was not until officers from the CWS began to testify that the subcommittee heard any arguments in support of a permanent, independent CWS. William L. Sibert, who was still serving as chief of the CWS, was the first to speak on August 25. Fries sat in the committee room with Sibert and occasionally interjected during his testimony. At the start, Sibert was asked about the testimony March had given weeks earlier and was invited to address whether or not gas warfare was inhumane, and whether or not gas could be researched without endangering human life.

Answering the first question, Sibert replied, "I do not consider anything that kills or maims only soldiers in war inhumane, because that is the object of war."[76] Inexplicably, however, he qualified his answer by saying that he would consider a weapon inhumane if it killed women and children "in a place which they had no reason to consider dangerous."[77] That response was very odd, since opponents of chemical warfare, such as March, frequently claimed that chemical weapons were inhumane because they did precisely that. As for the second issue, whether or not chemical weapons research was too dangerous to be undertaken, Sibert spoke about the same accident that March had described in his testimony. Sibert testified that while many experiments were conducted at American University during World War I, "we never had but one slight accident, and that was the case of ex-Senator Scott, who was slightly gassed."[78] He muddied the waters considerably, saying that it "was not due to the experiment that we were carrying on but to an accident."[79] It was unclear how he thought that this characterization mitigated the incident.

Fries was the next expert to speak that day, and his remarks were lengthy, offering relatively few pauses for questions from the senators. He spent most of his testimony explaining historical and technical information about chemical weapons to the members of the subcommittee. Fries also took time to address more articulately the two points Sibert had spoken to earlier. He suggested that gas was not only humane, it was indeed the most humane weapon of war available. "Gas is the only weapon of war against which you have absolute protection," Fries said, because a properly worn gas mask would protect you from all harm, and no such protective device existed for bullets or artillery shells.[80] He also expressed that civilians had nothing to fear from chemical-weapons research conducted in their midst. Fries said that chlorine gas is transported for commercial use across America's railways without incident, and that he lived safely with his family at Edgewood Arsenal, where two thousand tons of poisonous gas was stored.[81]

Fries attended the next day's hearing, when his associate Charles H. Herty was called to testify. Herty discussed the editorial efforts he had made on behalf of the CWS in the *Journal of Industrial and Engineering Chemistry*. He quoted from several of his own articles about the importance of the CWS and said that when he heard the organization was going to be eliminated, "I made up my mind at once that the chemists of the country must know the story. I selected from this testimony and this record this material, and I changed my whole September issue, and it is all here, an appeal to the chemists of this country to awaken the people of this country to what this proposition means."[82] Herty suggested that the establishment of a permanent CWS would signify that research chemists played an important role in national defense. If their duties were relegated to the Engineering Department, "the Chemical Warfare Service will never be what it should be in the Army," and Herty lamented that "it is going to affect the sprit of the chemists of the country."[83] Expressing open frustration with those who sought to end the CWS, Herty exclaimed, "This thing is so absurd in so many ways that I almost lose my patience talking about it."[84] Fries and Herty, and to a lesser extent Sibert, represented the first, and in most ways the last real support the CWS received during these subcommittee hearings.

Three days after Herty spoke, the Subcommittee on Army Reorganization called William H. Walker, former head of Edgewood Arsenal, to speak about the postwar conditions and manufacturing operations at Edgewood. Senator Joseph S. Frelinghuysen used his question period to harangue Walker about the threat that chemical weapons in storage could pose to nearby civilians. After establishing how much poison gas was stored at the Bound Brook facility in Frelinghuysen's home district in New Jersey, he asked Walker a series of pointed hypothetical questions: "What would have happened if the plant had been struck by lightning, or if there had been an explosion? What would have happened to the surrounding neighborhood?"[85] Frelinghuysen asserted that the neighborhood might "be subjected to loss of life and a great deal of suffering if an accident occurred," and he asked if Walker believed "it was right to keep a large quantity there for such a long time, subjecting the people of the community to danger?"[86]

Walker floundered against this verbal assault until Fries, who was present, interrupted the proceedings and began to answer Frelinghuysen's questions himself. He assured the senator that stored chemical weapons posed no danger to the general population whatsoever. Repeating his earlier testimony, Fries said that he and his family lived "right on top of it" at Edgewood Arsenal where thousands of tons of chemical weapons were stored.[87] Frelinghuysen made another attempt to disparage chemical weapons once the next expert, former CWS research chemist Frank M. Dorsey, gave testimony, but again Fries, not Dorsey, answered the questions.[88] Afterward, the senate hearings on the army reorganization bill continued for another month, but the subject of a permanent CWS was only approached sporadically.

During the army reorganization hearings, the witnesses who strongly supported an independent CWS, such as Fries and Herty, were outnumbered by those who were indifferent or who wanted to see it become part of an existing military department. The most senior members of the Department of War to testify, March, Baker, and other individuals of high rank, tended to support the end of the CWS. As is the case with congressional hearings in general, however, the reorganization hearings ultimately had no discernable effect on the legislation being considered. The bill that the subcommittee ultimately referred to the full committee established a permanent, independent CWS. The full Military Affairs Committee approved of the provision and sent the bill to the Senate, where it was also accepted. The 2nd Army Reorganization Bill was passed into law as the National Defense Act on June 4, 1920. Not only did the act allow the CWS to continue chemical warfare work, but it also contained a provision for Fries to be elevated in rank. The CWS publication *Chemical Warfare* explained that "it was the purpose of retaining Colonel Fries as chief of our service that the proviso was inserted in Section 4 of this act, allowing an officer of twenty-two years service to be placed on the list of those eligible for promotion to General Officers."[89]

Without the support of their superiors in the army, and in spite of all of the negative testimony that had been given during the subcommittee hearings, Fries and the CWS successfully managed to influence the political process by working outside of regular legislative channels. Fries and his supporters corresponded and met with members of the Military Affairs Committee while the bill was under consideration. Senator Chamberlain, in particular, was an important contact for the CWS because he seemed most sympathetic to their cause, and he and Fries exchanged letters several times during the hearings. On August 19, 1919, Chamberlain wrote to Fries that he appreciated "the suggestions which you make in criticism of my analysis of the Army Reorganization Bill, so far as it applied to a chemical bureau and to chemical warfare."[90] He went on in the letter to arrange a meeting with Fries: "I will be glad some time before any bill is finally formulated to go over the situation and get your matured views as to what ought to be in a reorganization bill as affecting the branch of the service which you have done so much to make effective. You need not fear that this legislation will be hastily acted upon."[91]

Fries was, therefore, in a very good position to influence the outcome of the reorganization legislation. During the hearings, Fries was able to use his influence with Chamberlain to suggest that Herty be invited to give testimony. "He is a very able man," Fries wrote to Chamberlain, "and one who knows the chemical profession and chemists of the United States probably better than any other person."[92] Chamberlain acted on the idea quickly, and Herty appeared before the subcommittee six days later.

In March 1920 Sibert was transferred from the CWS to Camp Gordon in Georgia, where he was ordered to serve as commander of the 5th Division. It was widely suspected among the supporters of the CWS that Sibert's transfer was punitive. They believed that the Department of War removed Sibert from the CWS out of revenge for the success they were achieving in the reorganization fight. This suspicion seemed to be confirmed when Sibert, after receiving official word of the transfer, retired from the army.[93]

Once Sibert retired, however, Fries received his well-deserved promotion. He became de facto chief of the CWS. "We regret the removal of General Sibert from the Service," the journal *Chemical and Metallurgical Engineering* said when his transfer was announced, "but welcome the appointment of Colonel Fries as his successor. It is essential at this time to have an intelligent, sympathetic, enthusiastic officer at the head of the service, and Colonel Fries embodies these qualities in quite as high a degree as did general Sibert."[94] The leadership that Fries had demonstrated during the army reorganization crisis would be needed in the years that followed, as the CWS worked to ensure the future of chemical warfare.

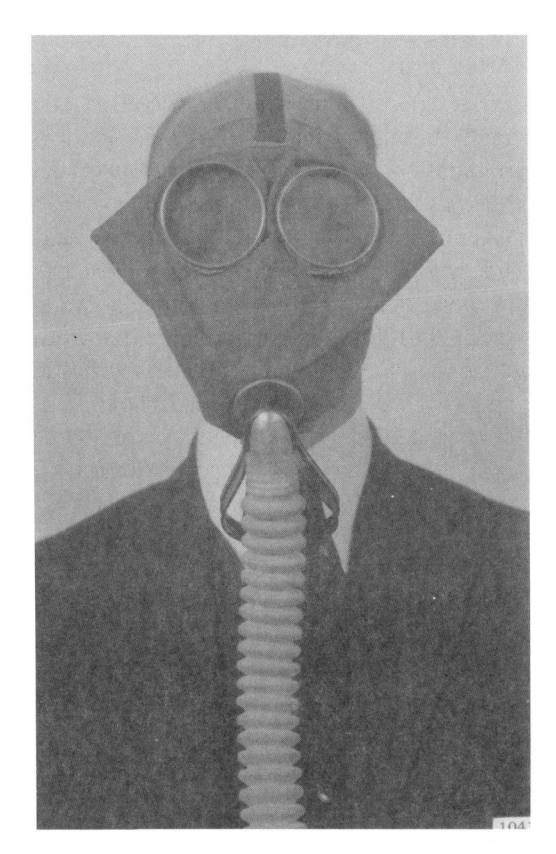

The wearer of this British-made Small Box Respirator (SBR), which was the standard-issue mask for U.S. soldiers during WWI, is demonstrating how difficult it is to see through the eye pieces when they fog. National Archives ("Development of American Tissot Type Mask," March 15, 1918, page 14, box 111, entry 46, War Gas Investigations, RG 70)

A French officer instructs U.S. soldiers on the wearing of the Tissot gas mask. National Archives (SC-111-4272)

Gas officer of the 35th Division demonstrating a smoke device. National Archives (SC-111-40834)

The 6th Infantry practicing maneuvers in their gas masks. National Archives (SC-111-159335)

A U.S. soldier rings an improvised gas alarm bell with the head of a pick ax. National Archives (SC-111-12148)

U.S. soldiers at the front react to a gas alarm: Verdun, April 30, 1918. National Archives (SC-111-11370)

Soldiers of the Chemical Warfare Service installing Livens projectors. National Archives (SC-111-161534)

Gassed patients from the 82nd and 89th Divisions awaiting treatment at a field hospital. National Archives (SC-111-22012)

Moving gassed soldiers into the bathhouse at the U.S. evacuation hospital in Baccarat. National Archives (SC-111-14646)

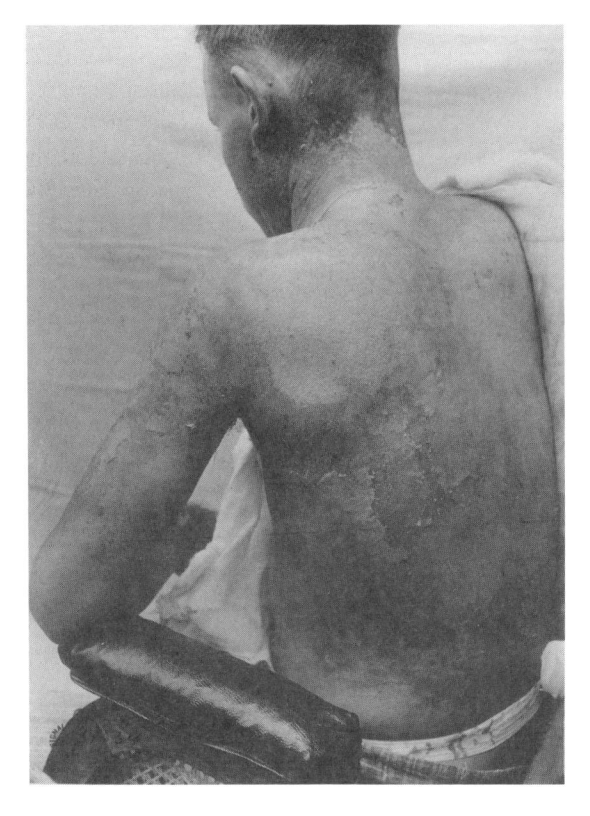

Mustard gas burns on Private Harvey Lawrence of the 130th Engineers. National Archives (SC-111-34034)

Soldiers preparing to use chloride of lime powder to disinfect a shell hole contaminated by mustard gas. National Archives (SC-111-35541)

Chloropicrin stills at Edgewood Arsenal for manufacturing tear gas. National Archives (RG 156 EA-1-1)

Automation at the Edgewood shell-filling plant: this machine paints colored stripes on shells to indicate what type of gas each contains. National Archives (RG 156 EA-1-1)

One area of the chlorine gas plant at Edgewood Arsenal. Said to be the largest factory of its kind in the world, it was only partially completed before the end of the war. National Archives ("Annual Report 1922," box 7, entry 4, Secret and Confidential Files, Records of the Office of the Chief, RG 175)

After WWI at Edgewood Arsenal, drums of phosgene and chlorine gas remain stored at an outdoor lot. National Archives ("Annual Report 1922," box 7, entry 4, Secret and Confidential Files, Records of the Office of the Chief, RG 175)

Chief of the Chemical Warfare Service Amos A. Fries in 1918. National Archives (SC-111-79153)

A roadside in France littered with discarded gas masks and other equipment. National Archives (SC-111-50122)

U.S. soldiers in France preparing to detonate several 77 mm gas shells after the Armistice. National Archives (SC-111-42817)

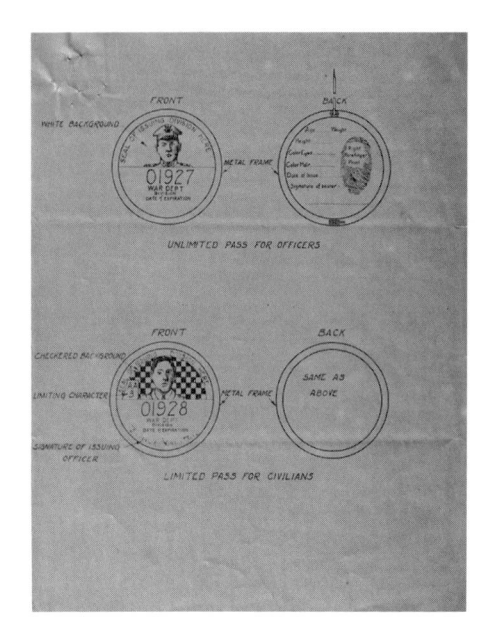

Identification badges for personnel and visitors at Edgewood Arsenal, designed in 1919. National Archives (Letter from G. Sevier, Colonel, U.S. Army Engineering and Standardization Branch, to W. W. Parker, Major, Chemical Warfare Service, Washington, D.C., May 20, 1919, folder: E&S Branch—P.S&T Division, box 16, entry 7, General Fries' File 1918–1920, C–E, Chemical Warfare Service, Edgewood Arsenal 1917–43, RG 175)

Diagram of a protective chemical suit developed by the U.S. Navy and U.S. Army Chemical Warfare Service in 1928. National Archives (Memorandum from B. M. Thompson, Lieutenant Commander, USN, Naval War College, March 8, 1928, Reference A, folder 727, box 45, entry 4, Secret and Confidential Files, Records of the Office of the Chief, RG 175)

4 Improvement, 1921–1925

The National Defense Act preserved the Chemical Warfare Service (CWS) as an organization within the military, but it was surrounded by army officers who still had doubts about chemical weapons. The tenuous relationship between the CWS and the rest of the military was exacerbated by the financial constraints of the postwar period. In 1922 Secretary of War John W. Weeks said of the army and its budget that "economy has literally become of primary consideration in every departmental undertaking."[1] The army's shrinking peacetime funds gave the enemies of gas warfare a justification for starving the CWS of money and resources. Rather than allow this, Amos A. Fries and the other officers of the CWS continued to build on the foundations they had laid during the army reorganization crisis. They cultivated relationships within the military and with civilians in the chemical industry to change perceptions of gas warfare and influence public policy. Changing public opinion in the United States with respect to chemical weapons was an important, long-term goal for the members of the CWS as they struggled to consolidate their gains and carry out their mission in the postwar world.

In the early 1920s there were several major indications that even though the CWS had maintained its independence, it was going to be rendered inconsequential by army leadership. In 1921, for example, the CWS fought with Chief of Staff Peyton C. March about preparing U.S. garrisons at overseas territories to defend themselves in the event that they were attacked with poison gas. Members of the Department of War harbored concerns about the precarious situation of overseas territories, such as Hawaii, the Philippines, and the Panama Canal zone, throughout the 1920s.

They worried that in the event of a surprise attack, these territories would be unable to mount an adequate defense and be overrun by a foreign foe.

As the U.S. Army and Navy worked to provide overseas territories with the means to defend themselves against conventional attack throughout the interwar period, the officers of the CWS sought to supply their garrisons with masks, and they trained personnel to protect them from chemical attack. The army chief of staff first considered the possibility of a poison gas attack on an overseas territory in 1920 and had approved a plan to send three officers and eighty-five enlisted men from the CWS to each of three overseas possessions: Oahu Island, the Philippines, and the Panama Canal. After a year, however, that plan had not been implemented. "When the time came to send these troops," a CWS memorandum explained, "the Chief of Staff directed that this be not done and a policy was adopted of concentrating all of the Chemical Warfare personnel at Edgewood Arsenal and confining their activities to research and development work."[2]

Once March retired in mid-1921 and John J. Pershing was appointed to replace him as army chief of staff, Fries recommended that a new policy be enforced. He asked that one department chemical-warfare officer, one administrative and supply detachment of six men, and one gas company of three officers and sixty-six enlisted men be sent to each overseas garrison. Pershing accepted this new proposal, but the reluctance shown by the Office of the Army Chief of Staff about an issue as essential as territorial defense was an indication that army leadership did not yet take chemical warfare especially seriously.

The relatively insignificant role given to the CWS in national mobilization plans was another signal that the army did not assign much significance to the matter of chemical warfare in the postwar period. Mobilization plans directed key elements of the military, in the event that the United States suddenly found itself at war, by describing where and how men and material would assemble and organize quickly.[3] Being a new military organization, the CWS had been left out of the plans in years up to 1923. Revisions made in both the 1923 and 1924 national mobilization plans included directives for the CWS, but the service was only permitted a very small, marginal force. In October 1924, as the national mobilization plan for 1925 was being prepared, the chief of the CWS argued that poison-gas soldiers should be allowed vastly greater resources and responsibilities:

> Various studies have indicated that a normal proportion of gas troops would be on a schedule of about one regiment for each Army, one battal-

ion for each Infantry Division, and at least one mounted platoon for each Cavalry Division.... The three regiments now provided in mobilization plans do not provide sufficient gas troops on the above basis; and the Chief of the Chemical Warfare Service expects to recommend the inclusion of additional units in the next revision of the Mobilization Plans.[4]

Fries envisioned a future war in which soldiers from the CWS would be attached to every unit in the army, directing offensive and defensive gas activities across the battlefield. Army planners provided for only a token force of gas advisors, however, and despite Fries's protests, the plans remained unchanged in 1925 as well.

The attempts made by the CWS to be substantively included in the mobilization plans of the early 1920s was a struggle that was neither as significant nor as protracted as the fight over the disposition of surplus gas masks and the state of the nation's gas-mask production capabilities. The gas-mask fight began when the rapid demobilization that followed World War I allowed the military to sell or store surplus chemical warfare equipment that would not be needed in peacetime and to close the factories that manufactured the equipment. Army gas masks began appearing in the marketplace as soon as the soldiers began to return from France after the armistice.

The members of the CWS were concerned about the fact that military gas masks were now being purchased by individuals and organizations in the United States. They knew that the masks had been designed to work with specific gasses under battlefield conditions, and they believed that the masks would be dangerous if they were misused by untrained civilians. Some fire departments, for example, issued the masks to firefighters even though they were not designed to allow wearers to breathe inside smoke-filled buildings. Miners, too, began using the masks under the erroneous impression that the filters would help them breathe as they worked underground. Both civilian chemists and the army tried to warn mask users against such practices.[5]

Alternatively, the CWS attempted to market surplus masks to chemical manufacturers and the metal industry. They claimed army masks were "admirably adapted to filtering out many chemical fumes and acid vapors from inspired air, provided the concentration of gas is low (less than 1 or 2 percent)."[6] That made the masks suitable for laborers in the metallurgical industry who were exposed to low concentrations of sulfur dioxide, in sulfite pulp and paper mills, or in sulfuric acid manufacturing plants. There was still apprehension, however, that the masks would not perform well even in those capacities. In the event of a poisonous gas leak, the concentration of gas inside a factory would be much higher than the concentration outside on an open field. Army veterans who might work at these plants were of particular concern to the CWS, since they had been trained to trust their gas masks on the battlefield and might not question the equipment's ability to function in the workplace.[7]

The CWS sought to develop improved gas masks and find new consumers for the modified designs. Unfortunately, grants from the Department of War following World War I did not allow them to do much research or development, nor were there enough funds to produce any new masks in quantity. As a result, most of the major improvements to gas-mask designs during the interwar period were made by private corporations and, ironically for the CWS, the Bureau of Mines in the Department of the Interior. In July 1921 the Bureau of Mines announced the development of an ammonia gas mask approved for use in mines.[8] Researchers at the bureau continued to improve the design until, in April 1923, they announced the creation of the "universal gas mask," intended for general industrial and commercial use.[9]

The CWS was also consistently denied the resources it needed to manufacture more gas masks and replenish the national reserve. Without new masks, U.S. Army soldiers would have to depend on the old ones held in storage if they faced chemical weapons in the future. The officers of the CWS knew that the military would not be able to rely on the reserve of aging and outdated masks that were beginning to deteriorate physically, and they pled the case during the National Defense Test Day demonstrations in 1924. Defense Test Day consisted of a series of well-publicized public demonstrations held at military instillations across the country on Armistice (now Veteran's) Day of that year. Ostensibly, they were designed to ensure that every level of the military was well prepared to defend the nation in a crisis, but the demonstrations were intended primarily to remind the American public of the importance of national defense.[10]

For National Defense Test Day, the CWS was ordered to hold a "parade, patriotic addresses and a field day," at Edgewood Arsenal, while "an inspection of chemical warfare installations [would] be made to determine our ability to properly carry on in case of emergency."[11] Fries and his officers were not content with this modest review of the nation's chemical warfare abilities, and they took it upon themselves to use this opportunity to spread awareness about the dangerous condition of the gas-mask reserves to the rest of the defense establishment. In August 1924 CWS Major William N. Porter wrote to the army assistant chief of staff, G-4, to complain that "the stock of Chemical Warfare supplies in depots at the present time is practically negligible. Procurement must, therefore, be arranged to meet almost the total of requirements."[12] Fries was more blunt in his characterization of the situation when he wrote to General Hugh A. Drum, G–3, in October. "I presume you know," Fries wrote, "that there are but some 8,000 serviceable gas masks on hand at this time in the continental United States, and no money in sight this year or next to make any more."[13]

Secretary of War John W. Weeks drafted an order that threatened to put a stop to the CWS's self-sponsored awareness campaign. Describing the objectives of National Defense Test Day to all participating officers, it read, in part, "It is further desired that you refrain from giving out detailed comments concerning the material side of mobilization and emphasize the personnel side only. Publicity should be accorded to individuals participating, particularly those of local prominence, as well as to local military units."[14] Since these military demonstrations were intended to improve public support for military preparedness, the elements of Defense Test Day that had human interest were of more publicity value than logistical information.

Even though Weeks had made his wishes clear, Fries continued to send memoranda on the subject of procurement to the Army General Staff (though he obeyed the letter of the order and does not seem to have advertised the state of the reserves to the general public). Fries expanded his criticism of the gas-mask shortage into a critique of U.S. chemical-warfare capabilities overall. He argued that financial constraints were forcing the CWS to close the manufacturing plants at Edgewood Arsenal, and that those factories would fall into disrepair over time.

> The gas mask situation is a typical example and one that presents the greatest difficulties but which could be easily corrected by the allocation of sufficient funds for the purpose. There are at present practically no masks in the Continental U.S. Reserve. In the event of war the production of the Edgewood Gas Mask Factory and two others of equal capacity would be required for more than six months to produce sufficient masks to equal the requirements for troops. . . .
>
> The problem of the Chemical Plants may be stated as even worse than the gas mask situation from a viewpoint of offensive uses. Sufficient funds are neither available for the building up of an adequate reserve of the products of the plants, or even for maintaining the most important of the plants in a stand-by condition ready for operation.[15]

After National Defense Test Day concluded, Fries returned to this subject in nearly identical language in his final report, but he also wrote that the day's demonstrations had been beneficial in many respects. His impression was that the demonstrations had promoted the idea of national defense with the public and "brought out the opposition in all of its phases enabling everyone who desired to find out the centers of opposition to proper national preparedness."[16] Fries suggested that National Defense Test Day become an annual event.

In the year that followed, the Department of War did not heed Fries's warnings regarding the condition of the U.S. gas-mask reserve. Throughout 1925 Fries continued to plead with the Secretary of War for gas-mask funding. When the Army announced its appropriations for the 1926 fiscal year in February of 1925, no funds for new gas masks were approved. In response, Fries authored a lengthy memorandum for Weeks titled "Desperate Condition of the Army in Respect to Gas Masks." It described the mask situation as a serious crisis for the CWS.

> Five years ago, lacking about one month only, and after [having] suddenly been appointed Chief of the Chemical Warfare Service, I went personally before Congress and urged the absolute necessity of making available enough money to manufacture at least one hundred twenty thousand new model masks. Two million dollars were made available and one hundred twenty thousand masks manufactured between July 1, 1920 and June 30, 1921. No masks have been manufactured for the army since that date.
>
> When masks for Panama have been shipped, the regular army in the United States will be as helpless against any kind of a gas attack as was the Princess Pat Regiment of Canadians in the first gas attack on the 22nd of April, 1915. Of the 120,000 gas masks, about 106,000 go to Hawaii, Philippines, and Panama, leaving in this country but 14,000, which covers three years use of such gas masks among Chemical Warfare Troops, the Chemical Warfare School, and all other troops, so that of the possible 14,000 available about 9,000 have been either used up by long service or are more or less worn from such use. . . .
>
> If there should be the slightest chance that our country would have to engage in war, it must have masks. Without them the nation is courting disaster.
>
> No nation is bound by any treaty or agreement not to use gas against the United States. . . . We are, therefore, today exposed to attack by gas from any country instantly and without any violation of any rule or agreement.
>
> . . . If we began manufacturing one hundred thousand per year, July 1, 1926, [the start of the next fiscal year] it would be June 30, 1930 before we could manufacture enough masks to give each man who would form the first front line a gas mask.
>
> . . . Our appropriations at present are so low that research on new compounds has had to be abandoned. Without question in the next year or two we will be completely outdistanced in research by Russia to say nothing of the greater powers.

I submit that this condition is courting disaster, and that the nation cannot afford to let this condition continue longer. This special report is submitted at this time before the budget for 1927 is made up. The situation is too critical to delay longer.[17]

Yet the Department of War delayed. With its peacetime resources spread thin, the army allowed the conditions described by Fries to continue in the years after the First World War. Fries alluded to an important reason the Department of War remained reluctant to fund chemical warfare preparations in his memorandum, when he explained that gas could be used "without any violation of any rule or agreement."[18] Delegations from the United States attended several international conferences in the 1920s where agreements to outlaw chemical warfare were discussed. The Department of War closely monitored the course of these discussions, unsure of whether chemical weapons would be successfully banned from future conflicts, and whether the CWS should be allowed to continue its work if chemical warfare became prohibited.

In November 1921 representatives of the victor nations of World War I met in Washington, D.C., for the Conference on the Limitation of Armaments. The attendees produced the well-known Washington Naval Treaty (1922) and another less-well-known treaty that never entered into force. Called the Treaty relating to the Use of Submarines and Noxious Gases in Warfare, it was intended to limit or prohibit the manufacture and proliferation of gas and submarines. The U.S. delegation, led by Secretary of State Charles Evans Hughes, proposed article 5, which read that asphyxiating or poisonous gas "having been justly condemned by the general opinion of the civilized world," would be hereafter prohibited "as part of international law binding alike the conscience and practice of nations."[19]

As the foreign policy arm of the U.S. government, the Department of State was the organization responsible for suggesting the language of international agreements relating to the future use of poison gas. The Subcommittee on New Agencies of Warfare that advised Hughes and the other U.S. delegates at the Washington Conference wrote that "on consultation with experts and reference to scientific study of the subject . . . there are arguments in favor of the use of gas which ought to be considered."[20] They acknowledged the low proportion of deaths to injuries when gas was used as a weapon but nevertheless concluded "there can be no actual restraint of the use by combatants of this new agency of warfare, if it is to be permitted in any guise. The frightful consequences of the use of toxic gasses if dropped from airplanes on cities stagger the imagination."[21]

The Department of State tabulated the letters and petitions it received from the American public from the beginning of the Conference on the Limitation of Armaments through January 15. They received a total of 385,170 petitions urging the abolition of chemical weapons, and a mere 169 urging retention with restrictions in use.[22] Therefore, the members of the Subcommittee on New Agencies of Warfare felt that they spoke with authority about American public opinion.

> The committee is of the opinion that the conscience of the American people has been profoundly shocked by the savage use of scientific discoveries for destruction rather than for construction.... Whatever may be the arguments of technical experts, the committee feels that the American representatives would not be doing their duty in expressing the conscience of the American people were they to fail in insisting upon the total abolition of chemical warfare.[23]

Faced with the likelihood that the future use of chemical weapons would be prohibited by the United States and other nations, the CWS challenged article 5 of the treaty after it was proposed. The organization asserted that a prohibition against chemical weapons could not, and should not, be enforced. Fries, who attended the Washington Conference as an advisor, wrote a memorandum to the U.S. Army General Staff listing several reasons article 5 should be rejected.

(a) Gas is an accepted weapon of warfare.
(b) It can be limited in its use against non-combatants only to the extent that other weapons of warfare are limited.
(c) The people of the United States, through the motion of Congress, have completely approved the use of gas in warfare.
(d) The United States, with its tremendous natural resources and great manufacturing industries, has an advantage in the use of gas over any other nation.
(e) The United States, being separated by oceans from possible powerful enemies, has its defense enormously strengthened by the use of gas.[24]

"Briefly," Fries summarized, "gas is powerful, effective, humane, economical. It therefore possesses all of the requirements of the ideal weapon of war."[25] He and the rest of the CWS believed that gas warfare was too superlative to be effectively prohibited by the international community or abandoned by the United States. There was also concern that ratification of the Treaty relating to the Use of Submarines and Noxious Gases in Warfare might put the CWS organization in jeopardy of abolition yet again.

After reading the proposed treaty language, Charles H. Herty once more rushed to the defense of chemists in uniform by publicly protesting international limitations on chemical weapons. Herty argued that prohibitions on chemical weapons could not be enforced as long as Germany and other foreign nations had the ability to produce poison gasses, and he proposed that Article 5 be replaced with language that prohibited chemical manufacturing in Germany. Herty and other American chemists wanted the Treaty relating to the Use of Submarines and Noxious Gases in Warfare to forbid the Germans from manufacturing chemicals such as commercial dyes and chlorine because factories that manufactured those materials could be converted into chemical weapons factories quickly in the event of war. Outlawing the German chemical industry by international agreement would also greatly benefit U.S. chemical manufacturers, who could sell more of their products to meet global demand.[26]

Delegates attending the Washington Conference did not accept the arguments made by the CWS and American chemists. Article 5 remained intact through the negotiations, and the Treaty relating to the Use of Submarines and Noxious Gases in Warfare was ultimately signed by the United States, Britain, Italy, and Japan. France, however, refused to sign, because the French delegation did not agree with the treaty's provisions regarding submarines.[27] Without France's signature, the treaty never entered into force, but the United States and other participating nations had agreed, in principle, to prohibit chemical weapons. Poison gas restrictions continued to be discussed at subsequent international conferences.

The attempt to prohibit chemical weapons made at the Washington Conference on the Limitation of Armaments understandably concerned the members of the CWS about the future of gas warfare. Fries and the other officers in the service appreciated a need to demonstrate to the Department of State, the rest of the military, and the nation that chemical weapons could, and would, be used in future wars. Consequently, they worked to be formally included in strategic "Color Plans" through the 1920s. The Color Plans were a series of war plans developed in the years between the world wars, for use in hypothetical conflicts with countries that were each assigned a color code name—red for Great Britain, black for Germany, orange for Japan, and so on, so that the names of the countries targeted would remain secret.[28]

Plan Green, which was the plan for a war against Mexico, went through several revisions during the 1920s. The Department of War evidently considered a military intervention in Mexico more likely than many other potential conflicts because Mexico was nearby, was undergoing a period of political instability, and had been invaded by the U.S. Army years before during the punitive expedition of 1916. As Plan Green was developed, the CWS exhausted a remarkable amount of effort trying to get chemical weapons included in plans for a future Mexican conflict.[29] Former chief of the CWS, William L. Sibert, said in 1919, "Should the United States intervene in Mexico, gas would be one of the most effective weapons procurable, at the same time saving much loss of life."[30] He believed that tear gas and other irritants would be ideal weapons in Mexico because "the more ignorant the people, the more likely they are to lose self-control and be thrown into a panic by gas, with its element of mystery."[31] The belief that gas was an ideal weapon against unprepared enemies was an attitude that was shared among members of the CWS but not among members of the Army War Plans Division. Fries was shown the most current version of Plan Green by a War Plans Division officer in 1921. The drafters assumed that the United States would sign the Treaty relating to the Use of Submarines and Noxious Gases in Warfare, and the plan did not permit any use of chemical weapons against Mexico.[32]

In 1922 Fries wrote a detailed memorandum urging the War Plans Division to give chemical weapons a much greater role in Plan Green. He expressed his view that the language of the Treaty relating to the Use of Submarines and Noxious Gases in Warfare did not necessarily prohibit the use of chemical weapons in all situations. Interpreting the treaty in those terms, Fries said, "will lead radicals to insist on the complete abolition of any preparation for defense against the unfair use of gas by a nation that might so use it if it felt it could achieve victory in that way."[33] If "radicals" in the country were to use the arms limitation treaty to abolish chemical warfare, then the country would be left defenseless. To prevent that from happening, Fries suggested adding language to Plan Green that would assert the U.S. right to use chemical weapons in most situations. If the United States went to war with a nation that had also signed the treaty, Fries proposed that the military should reserve the right to use chemical weapons in retaliation if the enemy used them first. Otherwise, Fries argued, the United States should make no promises regarding chemical weapons and should consider using them against all enemies in future wars.[34]

An army administrator, H. H. Tebbetts, authored a reply after receiving Fries's recommendation and completely rejected his suggestions. "The fact [is] that the commitments of the United States are opposed to the use of gases in any form in warfare," the letter read, "it is considered unwise to incorporate in Special Plan Green any reference to the use of gases, as this would obviously be opposed to public policy."[35] The letter went on to describe the rationale for omitting chemical weapons in more forceful language, saying that "it is inconceivable that the United States will initiate the use of gases under Special Plan Green, and [it is] by no means certain that it will even use them in retaliation. Aside from this, it is quite unlikely that the prospective enemy under Special Plan Green will invite retaliatory measures by using gases in any form."[36]

The opposition to chemical warfare within the Department of War was justifiable in the context of the time. As a matter of public policy, the United States was opposed to the use of chemical weapons. It was also argued, correctly, that Mexico was not expected to use chemical weapons against the United States in the event of war. Nevertheless, Fries and his officers were committed to chemical weapons as a method of warfare that future conflicts would depend on. They could not, therefore, accept that the United States would not use chemical weapons in a future conflict.

Members of the CWS searched for ways to convince the rest of the army that they should be included in War Plan Green. In late 1922 the CWS was alerted to a newspaper story that appeared in *El Universal*, a Mexico City periodical. It alluded to chemical weapons experiments the Mexican military was conducting on animals. According to the article, the gas they were using was "alleged superior," and rendered masks "of no protection against the gas, since the deadly effect is communicated through the pores of the skin as well as by inhalation."[37] This story seemed to confirm prior rumors that Mexico was developing its chemical warfare capability, and officers of the CWS began an investigation. If they could uncover proof that Mexico was developing chemical weapons, they could try to use the information to convince the Department of War to take the threat of gas warfare more seriously.

A CWS officer at Fort Houston, Texas, presented Fries with additional information about suspected Mexican gas warfare activities in a letter on November 1, 1922. He wrote that he had contacted an unnamed "agent" with knowledge of chemical warfare preparations in Mexico, someone who told him "the Government of Mexico had in the past purchased and is now purchasing gas masks in this country for use by the Mexican Army."[38] The agent also said that the Mexican government had been attempting to develop war gases by experimenting with poison plants. The CWS in Texas identified two plants they believed the Mexicans were using, one of which they called "gobernadora," which they said grew in large quantities in the mountains of Mexico and naturally emitted vapors that were "extremely poisonous."[39] "It is said by Mexicans," they reported, "that these vapors are so toxic that birds have been found dead under its branches, evidently having alighted in the branches."[40] The second plant was called "huichalienous," or "tetlatin," which was "considered far more dangerous."[41] They reported that this plant seriously affected human glands and could cause painful swelling, and even death. The CWS contacted the Military Attachés of Mexico and Venezuela as well as Wilson Popenoe, an expert on Latin American plant life at the Department of Agriculture, to gather as much information as they could about the plants.

In January 1923 army intelligence officers promised to ship samples of the plants to the CWS for testing. No record was found indicating whether or not these samples were sent or what became of them, but there is little basis for believing that these plants were being used in chemical warfare research. Gobernadora may be creosote, a hardy, flowering shrub that grows throughout northern Mexico and the American Southwest. Individual plants of that variety are sometimes found with "dead zones" around them where no other plants grow, but that is because creosote takes a lot of water out of the soil and makes it difficult for nearby plants to survive, not because it is poisonous. It is less clear what huichalienous or tetlatin is, but pharmacologists of that era noted a poisonous plant called Rhus tetlatin, in the same plant genus as sumac.[42] While the resin inside sumac plants can cause severe skin irritation, it is doubtful that the substance could be weaponized or mass produced in the quantities that would be needed in a war. Nothing came of the Mexican chemical warfare program, and this occurrence serves as an example of how a nation's chemical warfare preparations may not be as extensive, or as extant, as they initially appear.

In subsequent years the CWS continued to try to get chemical weapons incorporated into War Plan Green, but they tempered their appeals. When the Department of War undertook a revision of Plan Green in 1925, the CWS requested only that the plan permit the use of tear gas against Mexican troops, if needed.[43] George M. Halloran, a CWS officer at Fort Houston, wrote that he believed "it would be rather difficult to get a recommendation in writing to the War Department from these headquarters in regard to the use of tear gas in this plan," but he promised to try.[44] The CWS remained unsuccessful, and the Department of War never approved language in Plan Green that would allow the use of chemical weapons against Mexico.

The events of the early 1920s demonstrated to the CWS that elements of the military and the American public were hostile to their craft: reductions in CWS staff and funding, failure to remedy the gas-mask shortage, refusal to include gas in war plans against potential enemies, and efforts to outlaw chemical warfare by international agreement all indicated that the future of chemical warfare and the CWS was uncertain at best. Fries and his fellow officers resolved to continue to build associations with members of Congress, chemists, and personnel in other areas of the military. They hoped that improving these relationships would buttress the CWS and advance its agenda.

To maintain and strengthen good relations with Congress, the CWS began to host events at Edgewood Arsenal for members of the House and Senate. In March 1921, for example, the CWS welcomed a group of congressmen for a tour of Edgewood's facilities. "I was very much impressed with Edgewood Arsenal," Senator Irvine Lenroot said after the visit. "I shall favor the continuance of research and development work in this branch of military service."[45] The CWS also organized Capitol Hill events and demonstrations. During one week in May, the CWS and the National Research Council set up exhibits for public view in the House Caucus Room. The members of Congress were reported to be "practically unanimous in commending the chemical exhibit."[46]

Of course, the members of the CWS also continued to work in fraternity with their partners in the civilian chemical industry. In 1920, Fries acted to change the federal government's policy with respect to inventions created by scientists in military service. Under existing policy, the federal government held patents to new discoveries because the research that led to them was publicly funded. That served as a significant disincentive for talented scientists, who knew it would be impossible to profit from any discoveries they made during the course of government-supported research. Fries advocated changes to the policy that allowed inventors to patent their own discoveries, provided that they allowed the government unrestricted free use.[47] He hoped the new policy would make CWS work more attractive to civilian chemists.

The American chemical industry benefited from its relationship with the CWS. Businesses that aided national defense could use patriotism to appeal to consumers, and chemical manufacturers advertised the work they did for the CWS during the war, and afterward, as proof that they provided an essential national service. Chemical manufacturers repeatedly used this argument to motivate Congress to wrap the nation in a blanket of protective tariffs after the First World War ended. They hoped that tariffs would protect fledgling (and potentially militarily strategic) chemical concerns, such as the dye industry, from foreign competitors. Indeed, dye manufacturers promoted themselves as "the Master Key Industry" of national defense.[48]

Sibert, Fries, and other officers in the CWS offered their steadfast, public support to U.S. dye manufacturers throughout the 1920s. In October 1921, Fries testified before Congress that "all of our war high explosives, most of our war gasses, many of our most important medicines and our photographic chemicals, all of which are essential in war" were all byproducts of the dye making process.[49] The CWS and the dye industry together were able to persuade Congress to keep high protective tariffs in place after World War I ended. Fries believed that "chemical warfare can never be a real success without the earnest co-operation of the chemists, the chemical research institutions, and the great chemical industries of the United States."[50] "Just as in the past," Fries wrote in 1920, "many of the most valuable inventions in fire-arms, powders and other implements of war have come from private individuals, [and] just so in the future will come the great majority of new inventions applicable to chemical warfare. It can not be otherwise."[51]

The close cooperation evident between the dye industry, the military, and Congress led to public allegations of corruption and monopolistic enterprise. In May 1920 the DuPont Company denied an accusation that they had threatened Senator George H. Moses in an attempt to coerce the passage of legislation in Congress.[52] Such rumors were a result of the growing public apprehension about the influence chemical corporations wielded in government. In response to this public fear, Senator William Henry King instigated several weeks of Senate hearings to investigate the American dye industry for monopolistic practices and corruption.[53] Chemical warfare officers, including Fries, testified on behalf of the dye industry at the hearings, which ended in the summer of 1922 after no significant wrongdoing had been uncovered.[54]

Chemical companies and the CWS also shared a common interest in the long-term medical effects of poison-gas exposure. Some workers who breathed poisonous fumes in the manufacturing industry over long periods claimed that their employers were responsible for any permanent respiratory illnesses they suffered. The CWS studied these claims, along with those of veterans who complained of illnesses caused by poison-gas exposure on the battlefield. Veterans like Daniel Snively, who was gassed while fighting with the U.S. Army in France, maintained for years after the war, "I cannot say that all is perfectly well with me. Unexpected fevers come on at evening; my eyes are gradually dimming, and in winter I have extreme difficulty in breathing, due to a constant inflammation of the bronchial tubes and the respiratory apparatus. Mine is but one case in many that I know."[55] There was widespread speculation that exposure to poison gas caused long-term physical problems and made veterans more susceptible to the postwar influenza epidemic.

The officers of the CWS maintained that chemical weapons were the most humane weapons in warfare. Part of that argument rested on the belief that there were no residual effects from gas poisoning. The CWS, therefore, worked to invalidate allegations that poison-gas exposure caused permanent injuries. Fries contended in 1919 that "the lung appears to have much the same felicity for curing injuries from gas as the skin has for curing itself against cuts and bruises."[56] In 1921 the CWS published a statement in *Chemical and Metallurgical Engineering* that affirmed they did "not take much stock in the claims that there are delayed effects arising from poison gas."[57]

In late 1921, Veterans' Bureau Director Charles R. Forbes asked the CWS to assist him with the compensation requests his office was receiving from gas victims. Fries assigned the chief of the CWS Medical Division, Edward B. Vedder, to study Veterans' Bureau compensation claims and the injuries they alleged. Fries reported in 1922 that an "examination of over ten hundred applications for compensation in the Veterans' Bureau disclosed the fact that nearly one-third of the cases claiming compensation for tuberculosis attributed their condition to gas. The same can be said of many other diseases."[58] This number of claims, Fries stated, was further evidence that "conditions attributed to the after effects of gas have been greatly exaggerated since the first introduction of this weapon."[59] He suggested "a campaign to educate the people as to true conditions following gas exposure" to address this issue.[60] In 1923, Forbes was forced to resign from the Veterans' Bureau amid accusations of rampant theft, bribery, and negligence. He was eventually tried and imprisoned for conspiracy to defraud the U.S. government.

The CWS and its supporters were able to argue that poison gas caused no lasting injuries because of the lack of information that was available in the 1920s about the pathology of chemical weapons. Medical professionals of the period had difficulty discerning one respiratory problem from another based on the common symptoms they all presented. The spread of the influenza pandemic after World War I left many patients with persistent respiratory problems, and doctors could not accurately determine whether a veteran suffered from the residual effects of the flu or chemical weapons. Other veterans suffered from mental distress related to gas exposure that was even more difficult to diagnose. Because chemical weapons were a relatively new phenomenon, the medical community had not yet had time to adequately study their long-term effects.

Gas exposure can result in vision and heart problems, but the symptoms can take years or even decades to manifest.[61] The medical studies conducted by the CWS helped prove, erroneously, that veteran soldiers and factory workers who were poisoned by gas rarely experienced permanent injury. It should be noted, though, that most Americans were skeptical of elite opinion on this subject and continued to believe that there was a prima facie correlation between poison gas exposure and persistent medical problems in the postwar period.

Chemists of the era did not question the ethics of working with the CWS or promoting chemical weapons as permissible tools of war. On the contrary, they generally supported the idea of serving their country by using their skills to aid in its defense. World War I and the CWS's postwar struggle coincided with the evolution of chemistry in America from a strictly academic pursuit to a profession with a voice in national policy.[62] Scientists and researchers who had been part of the war effort believed that they should continue to play an important role in national defense after the war ended. "The problems of peace are inextricably entangled with those of war," astrophysicist George Ellery Hale wrote in 1920, "and if scientific methods and the aid of scientific research were needed in overcoming the menace of the enemy they will be no less urgently needed during the turmoil of reconstruction and the future competitions of peace."[63] In January 1922 the editor of the chemistry periodical *Chemical Age* wrote, "We do not severely criticize the attitude that demands further experiments in death-dealing. It is seen by its advocates as a means of precaution, of preparedness. . . . [W]e cannot avoid the conclusion that upon Science must rest the responsibility of feeding the agencies that war uses."[64] Chemists in Europe also held similar views about the scientist's responsibility for national defense.[65] Several chemical-industry associations in the United States debated and published codes of ethics through 1923. Those codes, however, described what chemists owed to science, their employers, and their customers, not what they owed to society more generally.[66]

While continuing to strengthen their relationships with civilian chemists and the chemical industry, the members of the CWS also sought to build support for their work among other organizations within the military. In 1921 CWS officer Earl J. Atkisson wrote a memorandum suggesting that the CWS and U.S. Army Ordnance Department collaborate together on a variety of projects. The Ordnance Department was responsible for weapons testing, procurement, and storage, and Atkisson believed that partnership was possible on projects "wherein the Chemical Warfare Service and Ordnance Department are mutually interested."[67]

Specifically, Atkisson proposed that the Ordnance Department provide the CWS with various pieces of military equipment for use in chemical warfare research. For example, Atkisson asked that the Ordnance Department provide every type of shell in use so that the CWS could develop chemical-filled shells for every model of gun. The CWS also pledged to test chemical weapons in airplane bombs, and they requested delivery of combustion engines used in different service vehicles so they could be tested to determine how well they worked in poison-gas clouds.[68] "The cooperation of the Ordnance Department with the Chemical Warfare Service in the development of gas warfare material is earnestly desired," Atkisson wrote. "It is felt that such cooperation to be effective must be extremely close."[69] The CWS had fought to remain separate from the Ordnance Department through 1919 and 1920, but now that the National Defense Act had affirmed their independence, the CWS initiated an extensive research collaboration that lasted through the 1930s.

One of the firmest alliances the CWS was able to forge with another military organization was with the burgeoning Army Air Service, the forerunner of the modern Air Force. Air warfare represented a relatively new type of war in much the same way chemical warfare did during the same period, and the two services had much in common.[70] Edward S. Farrow, a former CWS officer who became a chemist at the Eastman Kodak Company after World War I, suggested in 1920 that a relationship between the two methods of warfare would be important in the future: "I believe," he wrote, "that gas and military aeronautics will play the principal parts in the next war, which will be literally finished in the chemical laboratory."[71] The CWS and the Army Air Service were obliged to unite against the opposition both organizations encountered from the U.S. Navy during the 1920s.

The conflict between the U.S. Navy and the Army Air Service during the interwar period is an infamous one.[72] Through those years, the Army Air Service sought to consolidate all military aviation together in one independent air force while the officers who commanded the navy wanted to manage their own aviation program as part of their branch of service.[73] Army Air Service officers such as General William "Billy" Mitchell, and CWS officers such as Fries, accused the navy of obstructing military innovation because, in their view, the navy was not doing enough to prepare for aerial and chemical combat. The CWS and the Army Air Service both lobbied persistently to conduct tests on decommissioned naval craft in order to prove that their methods of war were forces the Navy would have to reckon with in future conflicts. They worked together because they believed that chemical weapons used against ships would most likely be deployed from above by airplanes.

In 1921 the CWS and the Air Service got their chance. The navy arranged for the Army Air Service to conduct a series of highly publicized demonstrations of airpower using several decommissioned warships as targets. In one demonstration, airplane bombs filled with phosphorous, tear gas, and other chemical weapons were tested in a mock-assault on the battleship USS *Alabama*. On the day of the test, observers watched as a single plane blanketed the entire ship in clouds of harmful chemicals.[74] Fries wrote that he thought the demonstration was entirely successful.

> The effect of the use of phosphorous bombs gave great promise for the use of this bomb, both to produce a covering smoke for the bombing areoplanes and also to produce casualties among the deck force by reason of the burning phosphorus scattered about. The effect of the tear gas bombs impressed everyone who went on board after their use, with the great possibility of the use of chemical agents from aeroplanes against Naval craft.[75]

Notwithstanding Fries's initial optimism, chemical warfare proponents continued to be dissatisfied with the Navy afterward. According to the editor of the chemistry periodical *Chemical and Metallurgical Engineering* in January 1922, "The Navy stands as a prejudiced party when chemical warfare is under consideration."[76] They had "shown few signs of progress and some evidence of a reactionary sprit."[77] The CWS and the Air Service continued to collaborate on projects intended to influence the navy's policies on new military technologies. In June 1923 Edgewood Arsenal hosted a demonstration of chemical smoke screens produced by Air Service planes. It was said that the experiment had "direct application to the use of coast artillery."[78] The *New York Times* covered the demonstration and reported the assertion of "one expert" that "if during the attack on the Dardanelles in the World War, . . . the shore batteries could have been blanketed by two or three airplanes, [then] there would have been practically no danger to the ships from those batteries."[79]

While the Navy continued to pursue aviation technology over the next few years, it did so at a pace that was too slow for the aircraft enthusiasts of the period. This led to a pattern of incidents that culminated in the wreck of the navy airship *Shenandoah* and the court martial of Billy Mitchell. *Shenandoah* crashed in Ohio during a storm on September 2, 1925, while on a publicity mission to demonstrate the successes of the naval air program. The crash killed the captain and several of the crew, and it prompted Mitchell, by then already the most well-known advocate of military airpower in the United States, to publicly criticize the national defense establishment and its neglect of rigid airships. Mitchell's subsequent court martial commanded the attention of the nation and involved the "who's who" of the U.S. military.[80] At the court martial on November 9, 1925, Fries was called as the very first witness to testify in Mitchell's defense. Fries described U.S. military vulnerabilities in apocalyptic tones; he told the court that a mere handful of planes dropping only twenty tons of tear gas could throw the city of Washington into chaos and force it to be evacuated.[81]

Mitchell hoped that Fries's testimony would convince the court that airplanes were a potentially devastating weapon of war that army and navy leaders had been neglecting. Fries hoped his testimony would also convince people of the same regarding chemical weapons. While Mitchell was subsequently found guilty by the court and forced out of the service, the CWS and the Army Air Service continued to collaborate on projects of mutual interest through the interwar period. In May that same year, the Air Service asked the CWS to design and supply them with gas masks to protect airplane pilots from chemical weapons.[82] The Air Service's patronage of the CWS that month and over the next decade was significant because it gave the soldiers of the CWS opportunities to prove their utility to other areas of the military.

As the officers of the CWS worked to sustain their organization and to argue that chemical weapons were indispensable and innovative, they supported an important and wide-ranging initiative to research new uses for war gasses in the early 1920s. Given the public's fear of chemical weapons, the CWS believed that researching and promoting the peacetime use of poison gas would help make it more palatable and improve the organization's public image. The idea that gasses designed to kill humans could have alternative, nonlethal uses may seem novel, but the members of the CWS were committed to using every resource at their disposal to get Americans to look more favorably on their branch of service. They managed to identify many potential applications in the field of pest removal. The CWS periodical *Chemical Warfare* editorialized that "it is very possible that our investigations will demonstrate that the quickest and surest method in attacking crop-destroying pests, whether ground squirrels, gopher, blackbird, crows, buzzard, rats, or grasshopper, is by cloud of gas."[83]

This proposition was not an easy one to make. Some war gasses were unsuitable for use against insects or animals because they were too dangerous to humans. Others killed plants as well as pests and could not be used on crops. Many gasses simply proved ineffective. In 1920 the CWS and partners in the Department of Agriculture tried, and failed, to find a method of breaking up crow roosts on farms using gas.[84] Subsequently, the CWS attempted to identify a war gas that would exterminate the boll weevil, but this time the Department of Agriculture publicly opposed the experiments and predicted that they would fail.[85] Because of the boll weevil's ability to suspend its respiration, the CWS experiments were unsuccessful and the insect continued to wreak havoc on U.S. farms until after World War II. Another unsuccessful research project conducted by the CWS involved combining poisonous chemicals and marine paint to produce a barnacle-resistant coating for use on boat hulls and marine pilings.[86]

Perhaps the most outlandish pest-control project undertaken by the CWS involved the use of poison gas in animal traps. The idea was attributed to inventor Thomas A. Edison, who reportedly thought of it while pondering a design for animal traps that used electricity to deliver "merciful and instant death."[87] He decided that such a use of electricity was impracticable, but he suggested to the Department of War that the CWS begin experimenting with poison gas as a lethal agent in animal traps instead. The method was promoted as safe, effective, and humane by Fries and fellow officer Clarence J. West in *Chemical Warfare*, a book they co-authored.[88] Though the majority of these types of experiments did not produce viable pest-control methods in the 1920s, they were important precursors to later, more successful innovations. The idea that certain types of war gasses shared chemical properties with fumigants was sound in principal, and even unsuccessful experiments helped convince Americans that chemical weapons and the soldiers who dealt with them could be useful. Eventually, practical insecticides were developed, and the CWS's pest-control initiative would stand out as one of their most well-known and successful postwar projects.[89]

Members of the CWS researched several other commercial applications of poison gas besides pest control. One of the stranger projects was brought to the attention of the CWS by a private inventor named W. O. Beckwith, of Fostoria, Ohio. Beckwith approached the service in June 1921 with a prototype of a device designed to protect post office safes from would-be robbers. The device was a container of poison gas and a small explosive detonator that could be affixed to the inside of a safe and rigged to release the gas if the door to the safe were forced open. A similar device had foiled a bank robbery in Michigan in February. There, three intruders were forced to abandon their attempt to rob the Farmers and Merchants' Bank of Utica after they triggered the release of a large quantity of mustard gas. The gas was so powerful that "it was a couple of hours before the building could be entered with safety" by police.[90]

When he heard about the invention, Fries wrote that he was "quite interested in this," adding that he was "sure many others in the War Department and other departments—especially the Post Office" would be interested as well.[91] He speculated about which poison gasses could best be used in the apparatus, writing that he "understood that in general it is not desirable to have a deadly concentration."[92] Fries immediately ordered his subordinates to arrange for Beckwith and representatives from the Post Office to meet at Edgewood Arsenal for a test demonstration.

> I would like to have this given the greatest attention because I am convinced that the protection of safes and strong rooms generally by means of gas will be common throughout the United States within five years. Whether Mr. Beckwith's schemes are the best . . . time alone will tell. However, any information we can get in the working of this apparatus will help us later.[93]

Fries' belief that poison-gas safe protectors would soon become common throughout the United States notwithstanding, the idea does not seem to have caught on. The CWS did hold a demonstration of Beckwith's invention the next month, and the investigating officers decided that with a few minor modifications the device would become useable. They passed their information on to the chief inspector of the U.S. Post Office but were promised only "that the matter will receive careful consideration."[94] Similar devices apparently continued to be used by some banks in the United States. In 1925 a group of burglars at a bank in Elnora, Indiana, were foiled by a device that released highly noxious lewisite. Following the thwarted robbery, the *Los Angeles Times* reported that other Indiana banks were discussing "plans to equip their vaults in a similar way with an antiburglar gas contrivance."[95]

Research projects that used war gasses in these ways suggest the lengths to which the CWS would go to prove that chemical weapons were useful and versatile. In 1924 and 1925 researchers in the CWS used pseudoscience in an attempt to prove that war gasses could be used as cures for common respiratory ailments. The idea purportedly originated with an observation made by the CWS at the large Edgewood Arsenal chlorine plant. During the influenza pandemic that followed the First World War, doctors there noticed that workers in that plant had proportionally fewer cases of influenza than other groups at the arsenal. This observation was meaningless at face value, but medical researchers in the CWS quickly concluded that the chlorine fumes in the plant must have been responsible for reducing instances of the disease among the workers.

Edward B. Vedder, the chief of the CWS Medical Division, and his subordinate Captain Harold P. Sawyer, conducted a series of experiments on patients with various respiratory ailments at the Edgewood Arsenal hospital. Patients with influenza, bronchitis, pneumonia, whooping cough, and common colds were exposed to nonlethal amounts of chlorine gas in test chambers. The treatment was continued over a period of several days and their symptoms were observed for signs of improvement. Vedder and Sawyer published their results in the *Journal of the American Medical Association*, where they concluded that chlorine gas could be used to cure lung infections.[96] Vedder later authored a more extensive article on the subject, published as "The Present Status of Chlorine Gas Therapy" in the *Annuals of Clinical Medicine*.[97]

Vedder was one of the U.S. Army's leading experts on tropical diseases and nutrition before his interests turned to chemical warfare during World War I. He became the director of the CWS Medical Division in 1922 where, like Fries and other officers at Edgewood, he championed poison gas as being "more humane than other forms of warfare."[98] The CWS trumpeted Vedder's chlorine research as a breakthrough in the treatment of disease.

A series of public-relations events were organized to advertise the healing power of poison gas. In May 1924 President Calvin Coolidge allowed the CWS to treat his cold with gas therapy, possibly at the suggestion of Secretary of War John W. Weeks. During his first treatment, Coolidge was sealed inside a gas chamber and exposed to low levels of chlorine gas for forty-five minutes. A representative of his administration told reporters that the president felt much better afterward, and that "all of the depression and lack of energy that accompanies a cold . . . had disappeared."[99] Coolidge returned for a second treatment the next day, bringing his wife Grace Ann to sit with him in the chamber while the gas was being administered. She did not have a cold but reportedly wanted to experience the process anyway.[100] After a third treatment on the subsequent day, Coolidge reported that his cold was gone.[101]

In the months that followed the gassing of the president, however, critics in the medical community repeatedly challenged the chlorine-gas cure. Many doctors appreciated that it was normal for the symptoms of a cold to go away after a few days, whether chlorine gas was administered to the patient or not. Opponents of gas therapy also found flaws in the research methods used by Vedder and the CWS doctors who originally developed the treatment. In January 1925, Fries publicly defended the gas cure after the New York Department of Health called the CWS's record of success exaggerated.[102] He referred to a recent publicity event in which the CWS gassed 23 senators, 146 members of the House, and 1,000 of their staff members, friends, and family in a committee room on Capitol Hill. Fries said that "no accurate record was kept of these cases," but he maintained that the majority of them were cured of their ailments by poison gas.[103] Later that year researchers at the University of Minnesota conducted a controlled experiment in which they administered chlorine gas to some patients but not to others, and they were able to demonstrate empirically that both sets of patients recovered at the same speed.[104] Once war gasses proved to be useless for treating respiratory infections, Fries and the physicians of the CWS ceased promoting chlorine-gas therapy.

The CWS had far more success promoting chemical weapons as a method of crowd control. Soon after the First World War ended, CWS officers recognized that police forces and National Guard units would find certain types of gasses useful as law enforcement tools. The CWS worked to develop tear-gas grenades and other nonlethal devices for use against large mobs and criminals barricaded in hideouts, but it did so initially under restriction. In February 1919 the Department of War expressly forbade the CWS from providing any military or civilian law-enforcement personnel with any type of chemical weapon.[105] The Department of War opposed the use of chemical weapons on civilians because of concern that gas would badly harm or kill its victims.

General Leonard Wood, a prominent officer and candidate for president, asked the Department of War to end its opposition to chemical crowd-control devices in the fall, when he led federal forces to suppress the steelworkers' strike in Gary, Indiana. Fifteen hundred soldiers from the 6th U.S. Army Division were deployed in Gary to restore order after five thousand workers at the U.S. Steel plant went on strike there in October 1919, and Wood requested that the soldiers be supplied with various gas grenades to pacify the steelworkers. In response, the Department of War reaffirmed the existing prohibition and informed all Army Department commanders that they did not want any chemical weapons used "against mobs composed of inhabitants of the United States."[106]

Law-enforcement personnel outside the military wanted the Department of War to reconsider this policy. A. C. Dillingham, the director of public safety in Norfolk, Virginia, wrote to Fries in September 1919 requesting information about gas grenades and asking if he could purchase them from the army. "We have had one or two incipient race riots," Dillingham wrote. "I have thought of using the fire engine for disbursing the mob, but better than all seems to me to be the gas bomb."[107] He added, "We do not want to kill these people, unless it is necessary."[108] Fries offered information about tear-gas devices in his reply but explained that he could not provide them. "Perhaps you are not aware," Fries wrote "that the War Department has issued a confidential circular that no gas or similar grenades will be used in riots."[109] While Fries could not supply Dillingham with tear-gas grenades, the two continued to correspond with each other about them through December.

The officers of the CWS worked to convince the Department of War to rescind proscriptions against tear gas, while they continued to design and test various crowd-control devices. Fries described some of the tear-gas weapons the CWS had developed in a letter on November 28, 1921: "We have developed a very satisfactory combination tear-gas hand and rifle grenade for use against mobs and possible native uprisings where greater force would not be necessary. We have also developed an emergency type 25-lb. aero bomb loaded with tear gas for use in dropping on roads, trails, and other areas which it is desired to deny to mobs or other unlawful gatherings."[110]

As they did with their other war-gas inventions, Fries and the officers of the CWS organized public-relations events to publicize their development of safe and effective tear-gas devices. In August 1921 a group of girl scouts from the Washington, D.C., area were invited to visit Edgewood Arsenal from their nearby retreat, Camp Bradley. "Through the kindness of General Amos A. Fries," a group of approximately sixty girls (one of whom was Fries's daughter Elizabeth) were given a tour of the chemical-warfare facilities at Edgewood.[111] The day's activities culminated in an event where the group of girls was exposed to tear gas. "The girls found that the name 'tear gas' was no misnomer as all cried copiously for a few seconds when the gas was released," the *Washington Post* reported. "They greatly enjoyed the trip and put it down as one of the red-letter events of the camp."[112]

In September 1921 the Department of War relented, revoking prior orders that prohibited the use of nonlethal gasses on civilians.[113] This decision coincided with the U.S. Army's intervention in a massive United Mine Workers strike in West Virginia that same month. A detachment of Edgewood Arsenal soldiers, armed with tear gas, was ordered to take part in the operation. The CWS personnel were never ordered to use the gas, however, and the strike was ended without chemical weapons being employed.[114] Afterward the Department of War demonstrated lingering concerns about tear gas, when the ban was briefly reinstated from January to July 1922. Policymakers worried that the terms being negotiated under the Treaty relating to the Use of Submarines and Noxious Gases in Warfare prohibited the use of crowd-control gasses. Once the military was assured that gas grenades were considered an exception to the treaty, their use on mobs was permitted once again.[115] The development of nonlethal crowd-control devices led to significant changes in U.S. military civil disturbance doctrine. In 1921 the CWS published the manual *Provisional Instructions for the Control of Mobs by Chemical Warfare*, which described different categories of mobs and the methods of pacifying each. The U.S. Army relied on CWS guidance and expertise through the 1920s as it explored methods of quelling domestic disorders without causing unnecessary loss of life.[116]

The CWS also indirectly fathered a method of capital punishment in the United States. In 1921 a deputy attorney general in Nevada, Frank Kern, successfully lobbied the state assembly to authorize the use of poisonous gas in executions. He argued that gas would be a more humane method of death than firing squad or hanging, the two other methods authorized in Nevada at the time. Early proposals for the humane use of gas in criminal executions included one that suggested condemned prisoners be gassed in their cells while asleep without warning, but thankfully that plan proved impossible, since witnesses would be unable to observe and prison cells were not airtight. Nevada instead constructed a small, specially designed gas chamber.[117]

A few months after gas executions were allowed by the state, a Chinese American named Gee Jon was arrested and convicted of the murder of Tom Quong Kee in Mina, Nevada. The court sentenced him to death by lethal gas. Gee appealed the sentence to the state supreme court and argued that death by lethal gas was impermissible under both federal and state law as cruel and unusual. The Supreme Court of Nevada rejected Gee's argument, ruling that the use of poison gas in an execution was humane and therefore did not constitute a cruel or unusual punishment:

> The revulsion on the part of many to the idea of execution by the administration of gas is due to an erroneous impression. The average person looks upon the use of gas with horror, because of the experiences incident to the late war. They forget that there are many kinds of gas, ranging from the harmless nonpoisonous tear gas, which may be used for the quelling of a mob, and the ordinary illuminating gas, which may produce painless death, to the highly poisonous gas which sears and destroys everything with which it comes in contact. It may be said to be a scientific fact that a painless death may be caused by the administration of lethal gas....
>
> We think it fair to assume that our Legislature, in enacting the law in question, sought to provide a method of inflicting the death penalty in the most humane manner known to modern science.[118]

Accordingly, Gee became the first criminal in America to be executed by lethal gas on February 8, 1924. Eventually, eleven other states would adopt the use of gas in criminal executions before lethal drug injections became the most accepted method. Gas executions and tear-gas weapons were both law enforcement tools made possible because of efforts by the CWS to change public opinion about chemical weapons. The science that the members of the CWS helped create, combined with the argument that chemical weapons were a humane method of warfare, provided both a means and a rationale for lethal-gas executions.

The 1920s was a decade of recurrent civil unrest in America. Changing social and economic forces after World War I fostered the growth of several reform movements that sometimes threatened order in communities across the United States. The army became involved in public disturbances whenever local law enforcement agencies became overwhelmed and called on federal military forces for aid. Acting as a civil police force was a role for the U.S. Army that many officers supported, inside and outside the CWS. They generally considered mob violence directly related to communism, and they likened communists to foreign enemies.[119]

Under Fries's leadership the soldiers of the CWS became enthusiastic warriors in the fight against communism. Fries himself was a vociferous anticommunist who spoke frequently at venues across the country about the threat that communists posed to the United States. Writer and social critic Norman Hapgood reported that Fries once lobbied the school board in Washington, D.C., to fire a teacher for writing a definition of socialism in *Forum* magazine.[120] In 1937 Fries published a book about his beliefs, *Communism Unmasked*, in which he wrote, "Communists are parasites who live as highwaymen live, by robbery of nations."[121] Fries argued that communists were adept "at deceit, and so use every good organization they can betray, cajole, bulldoze, or seduce into joining with them in their efforts to destroy governments."[122] He and his supporters hoped that CWS tear gas grenades would be a front-line weapon in the war against communist labor agitation.

Fries and the CWS were responsible for one of the most notable smear campaigns of the 1920s red scare. In December 1922, a librarian in the CWS named Lucia R. Maxwell began preparing a chart that listed the names of several women's political organizations and their leaders, illustrating their connections to each other. The spider-web chart, as it came to be known, purported to expose a vast conspiracy of women's organizations working together in a network that promoted Marxism and undermined the nation.[123]

Fries supported the creation of the chart, and once it was finished, he made reproductions and disseminated it to military and civilian agencies across the country. Newspapers, led by Henry Ford's *Dearborn Independent*, soon reproduced Maxwell's chart to make the general public aware of this insidious red gender scheme.[124] The organizations it listed as members of the international socialist movement included the Women's International League for Peace and Freedom, the National League of Women's Voters, the National Council for the Prevention of War, the Women's Christian Temperance Union, and the American Home Economics Association. The original version of the chart also included the Daughters of the American Revolution (DAR), but that organization's name was removed and the space was left blank in early published versions.[125] The notion that anyone would accuse the DAR of being involved in a communist conspiracy is laughable. Members of the DAR were known as reliable anti-communist crusaders throughout the 1920s. Additionally, Fries' wife Elizabeth was the publicity chairman for the DAR at that time.[126]

The spider-web chart, once it was publicized, caused a backlash against the CWS and the army. The groups mentioned by the chart, along with other sympathetic organizations, protested the smear and demanded that the periodicals and government officials who distributed it destroy their copies and apologize. Worse, many of the antiwar groups then in existence took their cue and began to denounce the military in general and the CWS in particular for their role in the controversy. Pacifists had mounted opposition against the CWS since the close of the war, but the publication of the spider-web chart focused and reinvigorated their protest. All of this resistance did very little to suppress the chart, however. While the organizations named in the spider-web chart were able to convincingly deny the existence of a feminist-Marxist conspiracy in the United States, the chart appeared and reappeared in various places and versions throughout the 1920s. It plagued the reputations of women's groups and damaged their fight for political rights.[127]

Since the passage of the National Defense Act in 1920, the officers of the CWS had worked diligently to improve their organization's standing within the military and to demonstrate that chemical weapons were useful and versatile. Yet in spite of the progress the CWS had made, chemical weapons still faced significant opposition from foreign-policy makers. In May 1925 representatives from several nations, including the United States, met in Geneva for a conference on regulating the international trade of arms, munitions, and implements of war. On the second day of the Geneva conference, Congressman Theodore E. Burton, the chairman of the U.S. delegation, expressed the need for "additional measures to deal with the traffic in poisonous gasses with the hope of reducing the barbarity of modern warfare."[128] At a plenary session two days later Burton expanded on his remark: "I cannot omit to express the very earnest desire of the Government and people of the United States that some provision be inserted in this convention relating to the use of asphyxiating, poisonous and deleterious gases. This subject has been brought to the attention of the Chief Executive, President Coolidge, and prohibition of the exportation of these gasses would meet with his express approval."[129]

Using language similar to that which had been incorporated into article 5 of the 1922 Washington Treaty relating to the Use of Submarines and Noxious Gases in Warfare, Burton proposed that international traffic in chemical weapons be completely outlawed: "The use in war of asphyxiating, poisonous or other gases, and of all analogous liquids, materials or devices has been justly condemned by the general opinion of the civilized world."[130] Although the ostensible purpose of the Geneva conference was to limit arms proliferation, several delegations expressed a desire to exceed that function and ban the future use of chemical weapons entirely, once Burton's proposal was made. A consensus believed that the only way to limit the proliferation of chemical weapons was to absolutely prohibit the use of poison gas in war.[131]

Earl J. Atkisson attended the Geneva conference as the CWS technical advisor; however, he did not arrive until several days after Burton's proposal had been made. When he reported for duty on May 11, Atkisson was surprised to learn that the abolition of chemical weapons was being discussed.[132] Although he had expected merely to advise the U.S. delegation on poison-gas limitation and proliferation, he rallied himself to oppose the proposed ban on behalf of the CWS. Atkisson worked within the technical committee of the conference to convince members of the U.S. delegation that limiting or eliminating chemical weapons was too difficult a problem to be dealt with in the current negotiations, and that the trade agreement currently under consideration was not an appropriate legal instrument for such a ban. This advice put Burton and the U.S. delegation in a difficult position. Though a number of their expert advisors were now making strong arguments against the proposal's adoption, the United States could not withdraw its own suggestion without losing face. To resolve the situation, Burton worked with the Department of State to craft an alternative proposal, suggesting that consideration of chemical weapons be moved to a separate gas-protocol amendment.[133]

Atkisson believed that the Department of State was undermining the CWS by endorsing, in U.S. foreign policy, the premise that chemical weapons were inhumane. The Department of State facilitated U.S. participation in all international conferences, and the CWS noted that since

World War I the department had not objected to the principal of outlawing chemical weapons on any occasion. The Department of State's representative on the legal committee at Geneva was Allen Welsh Dulles, chief of the Near East division and future director of Central Intelligence. In his report to the chief of the CWS on the Geneva conference, Atkisson expressed his personal impressions of both Burton and Dulles relative to the proposed gas ban.

> The Chairman of the U.S. Delegation is a grand old man, honest and sincere in the fullest meaning of those words. He is devoted to the cause of peace. He believes that chemical warfare is barbarous, and that enlightened public opinion will almost automatically do away with it. He was supported in this belief by instructions from the State Department. That he really knew nothing about the subject is not surprising. Mr. Dulles, directly from the State Department, undoubtedly felt that it was his special function to see that the State Department's instructions were carried out to the absolute limit of their intent and letter. He appreciated that it was the intent of the State Department to extend the provisions of the Washington Treaty on every occasion. He is a young man of limited experience, and wholly incapable of passing on the merits of a project intimately related to technical questions pertaining to national defense.[134]

Once the new U.S. proposal was accepted, the delegations at Geneva continued to negotiate the Gas Protocol. Its text, outlawing the export and wartime use of chemical weapons, was finalized on June 11, and the U.S. delegation signed it at a ceremony on June 17.[135] While the Gas Protocol did not expressly prohibit the development or manufacturing of poison gas, the CWS balked at the restrictions nonetheless. The United States had declared that it would not use chemical weapons in future wars, and had officially disparaged poison gas as barbaric in an international forum. The CWS feared that, over time, international agreements limiting the use of war gasses would affect their ability to remain a part of the military and would leave the United States vulnerable to enemy chemical weapons. Officers of the CWS also feared that the United States was surrendering what would be an important advantage in future wars. A captain with the CWS in the Philippines wrote on October 1 about the potential for the United States to wage "unlimited Chemical Warfare" against future enemies.[136]

> Gas will be the greatest aid to the belligerent whose resources in gas production are greatest. At the signing of the Armistice in 1918 the United States was easily the leader in this respect. In view of her resources in raw material and financial power it would be to the advantage of the

United States to use gas against any enemy or combination of enemies. Her vast productive capacity would insure that her troops could engage in unlimited Chemical Warfare day and night, summer and winter until the end of the war."[137]

While the U.S. delegation to Geneva had signed the treaty, it still had to be ratified by the Senate, and chemical warfare enthusiasts hoped that the Gas Protocol could be defeated there. The Senate began consideration of the protocol the following year, in 1926.

5 Legacy, 1926–1929

By 1926, the Chemical Warfare Service (CWS) had developed into a well-established organization capable of supporting the continuation of poison-gas work into the foreseeable future. The officers of the CWS had successfully influenced public policy to make it possible for chemical warfare research to proceed after World War I, and the Department of War was beginning to act more favorably on their requests and proposals. Despite what the CWS and its supporters had been able to achieve during the decade, however, they were unable to motivate people to believe that gas warfare was humane. Public hostility toward chemical weapons ultimately led to the successful establishment of international agreements prohibiting chemical warfare.

The Geneva Gas Protocol was officially submitted to the Senate Foreign Relations Committee by President Calvin Coolidge on January 12, 1926.[1] Secretary of State Frank B. Kellogg sent a letter to the committee endorsing the protocol, and Congressman Theodore E. Burton spoke in favor of its ratification at a hearing the committee held on June 26. The Committee on Foreign Relations voted to approve the protocol and to send it to the full Senate the same day. The Senate took up consideration of the Gas Protocol on December 9, and it was then that the measure began to face serious resistance.

After the protocol was introduced by William E. Borah (chairman of the Committee on Foreign Relations), James W. Wadsworth Jr. (chairman of the Committee on Military Affairs) spoke in opposition. During his remarks, Wadsworth restated many of the arguments against chemical-weapons limitation that had been made by the CWS and its supporters since the end of the First World War. He said that it should "be remembered that when war breaks out, treaties and conventions perish," because nations would defend themselves using every weapon that is "militarily effective."[2] He predicted that the Gas Protocol would therefore fail to prevent the future use of chemical weapons and would leave the United States at a disadvantage against enemies who chose to violate it.

Wadsworth also argued that poison gas was not inherently more barbaric or injurious than other types of weapons, and he offered statistics suggesting that soldiers who had been gassed during the war became more resistant to tuberculosis as a result. Senator George W. Norris interrupted Wadsworth at that point, and asked: "The Senator does not mean to say that gassing is a cure for tuberculosis?"[3] Wadsworth replied that he "had not made any such assertion," and that he was merely dispelling "the popular illusion that gas is conductive to tuberculosis."[4] Norris replied, "If those figures are absolutely correct they go even further than that."[5] Instead of responding to Norris, Wadsworth yielded to Senator David A. Reed of Pennsylvania, who had asked to speak. Reed said that he knew physicians from the Veterans' Bureau had concluded that chemical-weapons exposure strengthened the lungs and made a person more resistant to respiratory ailments; Norris did not speak again.[6]

After more debate, Reed asked the chief clerk of the Senate to print resolutions into the record that opposed the Gas Protocol, received from the Association of Military Surgeons, the American Legion, the Veterans of Foreign Wars, the Reserve Officers' Association, and the Military Order of the World War.[7] These resolutions asserted that chemical weapons were effective, humane, and necessary for national defense. While he was not a member of the Senate, and thus not a participant in the debate, on January 19 Burton expressed his belief that military organizations that opposed the protocol were ignoring the opinions of their members in order to advance the interests of chemical corporations in the House of Representatives. The director of the legislative committee of the American Legion, John Thomas Taylor, was also a CWS reserve officer, a friend of CWS chief Amos A. Fries, and treasurer for an industry-supported interest group called the National Association for Chemical Defense.[8] While Taylor's support for chemical weapons was far from definitive proof that the leaders of the American Legion had been corrupted by the chemical industry, Burton claimed that the "rank and file" veterans who had experienced gas warfare in World War I wanted the Senate to ratify the Gas Protocol, despite what these resolutions indicated.[9]

Borah decided to delay the vote on the Gas Protocol until the following week so that more of the senators who supported it could be present. In the interim on December 10, former Army Chief of Staff and Commander of the American Expeditionary Force John J. Pershing sent a letter to the Senate, which the chief clerk read into the record. Pershing wrote that he felt there was a perceived discrepancy between his support for chemical weapons during the First World War and his more recent support for international restrictions. He explained that he first agreed to support chemical weapons, against his personal feelings, because he believed they were necessary for national defense. Now, however, he believed that the United States should take advantage of opportunities to prohibit their use internationally: "To sanction the use of gas in any form," he said, "would be to open the way for the use of the most deadly gasses and the possible poisoning of whole populations of noncombatant men, women, and children. The contemplation of such a result is shocking to the senses. It is unthinkable that civilization should decide on such a course.[10]

Debate resumed on Monday, December 13, and several supporters of the Gas Protocol made arguments in favor of its ratification. Senator James Thomas Heflin said he believed poison gas to be "a brutal and horrible method of warfare," and he mentioned that his nephew suffered permanent injury from gas during World War I.[11] He was interrupted several times by laughter in the Senate chamber as he mocked the "friends" of poison gas, and he suggested that if chemical weapons were so "delightful" that they "bring some of this mild-mannered poison gas here for Senators to inhale."[12] Representative Hamilton Fish III, who had served as a captain in the 369th Infantry Regiment during World War I, sent a stirring letter to the Senate urging ratification of the Gas Protocol, stating that approval of the Gas Protocol would save lives and prevent needless suffering. He asked the Senate to "strike a powerful blow at this new weapon of destruction before it becomes the abomination and desolation of modern civilization."[13]

Nevertheless, the Gas Protocol's opponents remained committed to defeating it. Sensing that he lacked the necessary support, Borah asked that the protocol be referred back to his Committee on Foreign Relations that day, without a vote, which effectively killed the measure.[14] The Senate's failure to ratify the Gas Protocol was partly due to the same postwar-era reluctance to enter into international agreements that had kept the United States from joining the League of Nations. The CWS also deserved some blame for the measure's demise, because the pro-gas arguments they had popularized helped the treaty's opponents to defeat it. Despite how unpopular the idea of chemical warfare remained in the United States and the international community, some senators believed that the potential disadvantages of the protocol outweighed its advantages. The Senate's marginalization of the Gas Protocol allowed officers of the CWS to claim, with veracity, that they were "not bound by any international agreement respecting Chemical Warfare" through the 1930s.[15] "Each disarmament conference at Geneva since the World War has agreed upon little except the prohibition of chemical warfare," CWS officer Adelno Gibson wrote in 1933: "Our delegation has in each case signed the agreement but in no case has our Senate ratified their action."[16]

After the Geneva Gas Protocol failed to be ratified, the CWS entered a period of sustained accomplishment. CWS officers commenced work on several new chemical-weapons initiatives in partnership with other departments and branches of the military, beginning with an effort to improve U.S. coastal defenses in 1927. The CWS maintained that shore batteries, which were installed to defend major ports along the nation's coast and at overseas possessions like the Panama Canal and Manila Harbor in the Philippines, were vulnerable to chemical attack. These batteries were fortified so that they would be able to withstand heavy naval gunfire, but the human crews inside could be exposed to poison gas if it were used against them.[17]

The Department of War supported CWS efforts to gas-proof costal defenses and allowed the CWS to conduct a field test at Fort Monroe, Virginia, in partnership with the navy. CWS officers hung chemically treated cloths and installed a ventilation system inside Battery De Russey at Fort Monroe, and the navy fired a live shell at the battery to test the integrity of the system.[18] The test demonstrated that the gas-proofing system was inadequate, but that result should not have been surprising. The heavy explosive shells that warships could fire at shore batteries should theoretically have been able to shake and shatter any cloth tarps or ventilator filters that the CWS could install. Explosions that could rip apart ship armor would naturally render any structure vulnerable to a poison gas attack. The fact that the Department of War committed resources to the project demonstrates the strength of support the CWS enjoyed within the military. They were allowed to continue experimenting with methods of gas-proofing Battery De Russey through 1932.[19]

The navy worked together with the CWS on projects of mutual interest far more often than in previous years. In 1927 the navy requested that the CWS begin developing a gas mask specifically designed for aviators, and they agreed to furnish 100 percent of the cost of development, an estimated $7,500.[20] In 1928 the army and the navy worked jointly with the CWS on the development of a rubber-like, pressurized full-body suit for aviators that would protect them from chemical clouds.[21] The suit was designed with a gas-mask face piece and a ventilation system that allowed breathable air to enter. The CWS also considered whether or not the suit could be issued to ground troops in combat to protect them from liquid agents like mustard gas and lewisite, but they concluded such a use would be impractical.

CWS researchers worked on several other significant projects during this period. A traveling exhibit of chemical warfare activities that the CWS assembled in 1927 featured many of the chemicals and equipment their scientists had developed, with varied levels of success, since the end of the war, including tear gas, pesticides, and marine piling paint.[22] One of the most important accomplishments on display was the work that the CWS had done in the field of smoke creation. The exhibit boasted that "the Chemical Warfare Service is probably the only scientific organization in this country studying the controlled production of smokes with special reference to smoke materials, methods of production and smoke cloud travel."[23] Smoke clouds had a variety of potential uses on the battlefield. They could provide cover for advancing soldiers, confuse an enemy, or assist airplanes looking for downed aviators. The development of smoke-producing chemicals was particularly significant for the field of military aviation. "Since the war, the development of air forces has still further enhanced the value of obscuring smoke," CWS officer Augustin Prentiss wrote in his book *Chemical Warfare*: "For not only are airplanes a means par excellence for putting down smoke screens on the field of battle, but their power of observation has greatly increased the need for obscuration."[24]

The Department of War's evolving attitude toward the CWS is also evident in their gradual inclusion of chemical weapons in war planning during the late 1920s. In 1927 the army and navy jointly conducted a series of war game exercises around Manila Bay that included simulated gas attacks.[25] The Department of War also began to amend many of the nation's war plans to include provisions for the offensive use of chemical weapons. In the summer of 1928, Plan Yellow, for example, was revised to include scenarios where chemical weapons would be deployed against the presumptive enemy.[26] War Plan Yellow was a planned response to a hypothetical Boxer-style rebellion in China.

As the Department of War considered the possibility that chemical weapons might be used in future wars, they gradually turned more attention to the issue of gas-mask development in the United States. In 1926 the Mine Safety Appliances Company in Pittsburgh asked the CWS for permission to "manufacture gas masks of the Navy and Army types for the governments of Brazil and Norway respectively."[27] CWS chief Fries endorsed this request because he "believed that the more gas masks that are made in the U.S. for foreign governments, the more advanced will be the knowledge of gas mask manufacture in the United States, which will be extremely useful and valuable to this country in case of emergency."[28] He sought and received approval from the Army Adjutant General's Office. Permitting other nations to purchase gas masks in the United States was a good policy for the CWS, since it would advance U.S. understanding of gas mask manufacture at no cost, however there was a growing need for the Department of War to manufacture its own gas masks to replenish the national reserve.

On March 21, 1927, the gas masks of the U.S. war reserve held at Schofield Barracks in Hawaii were inspected by the CWS.[29] Those masks had been manufactured nine years earlier, during World War I, and were stored at Schofield afterward in case Hawaii faced an enemy chemical attack. CWS officers selected ten boxes from various places in the storage pile, opened them, and carefully inspected the twenty masks inside each box. They found a number of deficiencies. The rubber face pieces were intact for the most part, though some were found stuck to each other and had to be pulled apart. Permanent kinks had formed in some of the masks and hoses where they had settled in the boxes. Some eyepieces were damaged "due to the cement between the lense having changed in some way to obscure the vision."[30] The far more serious problems, unfortunately, had to do with their air valves. Some of the flutter valves that were inspected showed signs of hardening, and the intake valves on some of the filter canisters were becoming hard and brittle.

These discoveries added to a growing body of evidence that the storage methods being used for gas masks were inadequate over long periods. Air valves seemed particularly affected by age in Hawaii and the continental United States, but rubber parts like hoses and face pieces deteriorated rapidly in the warmer, more humid climates of Panama and the Philippines.[31] Any type of damage to a gas mask could prove fatal to a wearer during a chemical attack. The CWS had warned the Department of War repeatedly through the 1920s that, in their estimation, the number of masks in the national reserve was insufficient to protect the army in the event of a war. Not only had no new masks been manufactured, but now it seemed that the existing reserve masks were gradually becoming unusable.

In 1928 the Department of War took action. Secretary of War Dwight F. Davis issued an order that changed department policy with respect to the CWS. It read, "The following which has been approved by the Secretary of War is furnished for your information and guidance: That it be the policy to protect War Reserve depot stocks of the Chemical Warfare

Service from deterioration and to include funds for this purpose in the estimate each year."³² Receiving Davis's authorization to maintain the gas-mask reserve and the promise of funds to do so was an important validation of the work that Fries and the other officers of the CWS had been doing to promote chemical warfare over the previous decade.

Army regulations required Fries to rotate out as CWS chief in 1929, and rather than accept a new assignment, he retired.³³ The dynamic and determined founding father of the CWS left behind an impressive list of accomplishments. Under his leadership, the CWS had adeptly maneuvered the policy process and improved impressions of chemical weapons among political and military elites in order to remain a consolidated and permanent organization after World War I. Its researchers had created new methods of pest control and crowd control and had made gas-defensive measures a military priority. The CWS had brought scientists, businessmen, soldiers, and national policymakers together in the service of the same cause, foreshadowing the collaboration that President Dwight Eisenhower would later term the military industrial complex.³⁴

But what the members of the CWS were able to accomplish must be considered in light of their failure to win public acceptance of chemical arms as weapons of war. Representatives of the United States had pursued foreign policies designed to limit chemical weapons throughout the 1920s, with the conviction that a majority of the public feared and detested chemical warfare. Despite the efforts of the CWS, the United States and its foreign allies persisted in crafting agreements designed to limit or prohibit the trade, manufacture, and use of poison gasses. The CWS itself, however, was partially to blame. The public relations campaign that sustained the organization also kept the subject of chemical weapons on the public agenda and sowed the seeds of popular censure.³⁵ Chemical warfare officers claimed that poison gas was a weapon that would win wars because they believed that, in the future, opposing armies would gas each other extensively with even more advanced poisons. This prediction was expected to convince people that chemical weapons were too important to be neglected, but instead it motivated them to support international limitations on those weapons.

After 1929, the United States continued to support international efforts to prevent chemical warfare. In 1932 U.S. delegates attended the World Disarmament Conference at Geneva, where they helped to craft an agreement that established, once again, that all future use of chemical weapons in war must be prohibited.³⁶ Those negotiations collapsed with the rise of fascism in Europe and the beginning of World War II. When the United States went to war in 1941, the CWS believed that Germany would use poison gas as it had done in World War I, and its officers urged the Department of War to make preparations. CWS personnel also argued that the United States should use chemical weapons offensively because, as chief of the CWS William N. Porter wrote, "no weapon would be too bad to stop or defeat Hitler."[37] Throughout World War II, however, the U.S. Army and Navy avoided the use of chemical weapons.

In a statement warning the Axis powers against using poison gas on June 8, 1943, President Franklin Roosevelt called chemical weapons inhumane and made it the policy of the United States not to use them except in retaliation. "I have been loath to believe that any Nation, even our present enemies," Roosevelt said, "could or would be willing to loose upon mankind such terrible and inhumane weapons."[38] "Use of such weapons," he continued, "has been outlawed by the general opinion of civilized mankind. This country has not used them, and I hope that we never will be compelled to use them. I state categorically that we shall under no circumstances resort to the use of such weapons unless they are first used by our enemies."[39] None of the Allies used chemical weapons during World War II, nor did Nazi Germany deploy poison gas in combat. While the reasons that chemical weapons were not used are still the subject of speculation, it is likely that no nation wanted to invite retaliation by using gas first, and in many cases the various fighting fronts moved too rapidly to make gas attacks effective.[40]

In the years that followed World War II, and after the bombing of Hiroshima and Nagasaki, atomic weapons faced an analogous situation to what the chemical weapons program encountered in the 1920s. To combat negative views of the U.S. atom-bomb program, President Eisenhower's administration launched the Atoms for Peace initiative that emphasized the nonmilitary applications of nuclear technology in domestic and foreign policy.[41] Atoms for Peace put atomic technology to work in power plants in the United States and other Western nations in a kind of nuclear Marshall Plan.[42] By promoting the peaceful uses of the atom, policymakers were able to strengthen U.S. political hegemony even as other nations developed their own nuclear technology. Atoms for Peace was a success, and nuclear weapons remained an important part of the nation's arsenal, even as the elimination of chemical weapons was discussed through most of the twentieth century.

The CWS was re-designated as the U.S. Army Chemical Corps after World War II and remained relatively inactive through the Korean War. During the U.S. war in Vietnam, the Chemical Corps made a variety of important, though unpopular, contributions through its work with defoliants, incendiaries, and riot-control chemicals.[43] The public's reaction to the military's use of these chemical agents, combined with a growing concern for the environment, effectively revived interest in prohibiting chemical weapons in the United States. On November 25, 1969, President Richard Nixon unilaterally affirmed that the United States would not use chemical and biological weapons in war unless such weapons were first used by an enemy, and he pledged the eventual destruction of existing chemical stockpiles.[44] Nixon also resubmitted the 1925 Geneva Gas Protocol to the Senate, and it was unanimously approved in 1974. To date, the protocol is still in force, and 137 countries have signed it. The U.S. Army again attempted to end the Chemical Corps as an area of service in 1973, but Congress intervened to prevent its abolition.[45]

In 1990 the United States and USSR signed a bilateral accord that required both nations to destroy their chemical weapons and prohibited them from manufacturing more in the future. Both nations also agreed to submit to inspections to verify that the terms of the accord were being met.[46] Afterward the United States supported the creation of the United Nations Chemical Weapons Convention, a multilateral treaty that required all of the ratifying nations to eliminate their chemical warfare capability. Currently, the U.S. military continues to destroy the nation's remaining chemical weapons in accordance with these international agreements.[47]

The CWS of the 1920s believed that future wars would be fought with chemical weapons even if international prohibitions were in place, because enemy armies were expected to use the most sophisticated weapons against each other regardless of what treaties were in force. Fries predicted in 1920 that chemical warfare agreements would ultimately prove to be unsustainable.

> Notwithstanding the bitter denunciation of chemical warfare as inhuman, it is believed that the calm judgment of the present and future will recognize that its use was a logical development of this scientific age. War being the ultimate expression of the passions in man and the final arbiter of all disputes, has from the beginning and will continue, rules or no rules, to take advantage of any weapon or other means that promises victory. Treaties will come and treaties will go as in the past, their provisions being violated under one pretext or another, as the exigencies of war demand or as the developments of trade and other peaceful pursuits appear advisable to the nations engaging therein.[48]

Far from the failure that Fries anticipated, the international community's attempts to limit the use of chemical weapons have been an overwhelming success. Poison gas is not considered a conventional weapon, and groups who practice chemical warfare have been marginalized as rogue nations and terrorists. The argument that poison gas was a key element of national defense, and the humane alternative to projectile weapons, found supporters among some policymakers in branches of the military, the scientific community, and Congress after World War I. However, the CWS was never able to persuade large groups of the public that a robust chemical-weapons program deserved support, and most Americans retained their preexisting, negative opinions about poison gas. Perhaps if the CWS were to have had effectively used chemical weapons against an enemy in a subsequent war, it is possible that poison gas could have become more generally accepted and been incorporated into the battlefield doctrine of the world's superpowers. Instead, chemical weapons have continued to be regarded as barbaric, and U.S. policymakers have prohibited rather than promoted their use.

NOTES

Introduction

1. The following account of this battle is based on E. W. Spencer, "The History of Gas Attacks upon the American Expeditionary Forces during the World War" (typescript, 1928), 194–95, U.S. Army Heritage and Education Center.
2. Ibid., 195.
3. Ibid., 194.
4. Fries and West, *Chemical Warfare*, 116.
5. Ibid.
6. Ibid.
7. Ibid.
8. While the British Army's chemical warfare effort during World War I is the subject of several English-language studies, books about the U.S. chemical warfare program have been far less profuse and comprehensive. Examples of recent books about the British chemical warfare program include: Richter, *Chemical Soldiers*; Palazzo, *Seeking Victory*; Girard, *Strange and Formidable Weapon*.
9. E. J. Atkisson, Major, Chemical Warfare Service, "Report on Chemical Warfare in Connection with the Conference for the Control of the International Trade in Arms, Munitions and Implements of War. Geneva, Switzerland, May–June, 1925," page 4, folder 319.1-1997, box 9, entry 4, Secret and Confidential Files, Records of the Office of the Chief, RG 175.
10. Fries, "The Chemical Warfare Service."
11. "Chemical Warfare Service," [October 16, 1919], 4.
12. Fries, "The Chemical Warfare Service."

Chapter 1. Origins, 1917

1. Bruce, *Lincoln and the Tools of War*, 247–48.
2. Hilmas, Smart, and Hill, "History of Chemical Warfare," in Tuorinsky, *Medical Aspects*, 11–12.
3. *Conventions and Declarations*, II.
4. Ibid.
5. Ibid., III.
6. Hilmas, Smart, and Hill, "History of Chemical Warfare," 12–14.
7. Ibid., 14–15.
8. "Cloud of Chlorine Borne by a Favoring Wind Germany's Novel Weapon

That Swept Allies' Front; Was Released from Bottles of the Liquefied Gas," *New York Times*, April 26, 1915.

9. Hilmas, Smart, and Hill, "History of Chemical Warfare," 15.

10. "[General] French Condemns the Use of Gas," *New York Times*, July 12, 1915.

11. "Russian Press Horrified," *New York Times*, May 11, 1915.

12. For British chemical warfare program in World War I, see Richter, *Chemical Soldiers*; Palazzo, *Seeking Victory*; Girard, *Strange and Formidable Weapon*.

13. Harris and Paxman, *Higher Form of Killing*, 13–17; Hilmas, Smart, and Hill, "History of Chemical Warfare," 18–19.

14. Hilmas, Smart, and Hill, "History of Chemical Warfare," 19.

15. Harris and Paxman, *Higher Form of Killing*, 19–21; Hilmas, Smart, and Hill, "History of Chemical Warfare," 19–20.

16. Cook, *No Place to Run*, 215.

17. Richter, *Chemical Soldiers*, 169–71, 193–94.

18. Palazzo, *Seeking Victory*, 103.

19. Heller, "Perils of Unpreparedness," 15.

20. Crowell, *America's Munitions*, 410.

21. Heller, *Chemical Warfare*, 35, 97n1.

22. Crowell, *America's Munitions*, 410.

23. West, "Chemical Warfare Service," in Yerkes, *New World of Science*, 149.

24. Heller, "Perils of Unpreparedness," 16.

25. "Historical Report to the Secretary of the Interior on the Origin and Development of the Research Work of the Bureau of Mines on Gases Used in Warfare, February 1, 1917, to March 1, 1918," folder 1, box 110, entry 46, War Gas Investigations, Reports, and Other Records, RG 70.

26. Ibid.

27. Ibid.

28. Burrell, "Research Division," 94.

29. *The National in the World War*, 163.

30. "Memorandum on Bureau of Mines Gas War Work," June 3, 1918, folder 1, box 110, entry 46, War Gas Investigations, RG 70.

31. Haber, *Poisonous Cloud*, 107.

32. "Historical Report . . . February 1, 1917, to March 1, 1918."

33. Parsons, "American Chemist in Warfare," 776.

34. "Dr. C. L. Parsons, A Noted Chemist," *New York Times*, February 15, 1954.

35. Parsons, "American Chemist in Warfare," 776.

36. *National in the World War*, 173.

37. Ibid.

38. "Historical Report . . . February 1, 1917 to March 1, 1918."

39. *The National in the World War*, 173.

40. Lamb, Wilson, and Chaney, "Gas Mask Absorbents"; Fries and West, *Chemical Warfare*, 237–71.

41. Crowell, *America's Munitions*, 417.

42. Ibid., 414–15.

43. Ibid., 416.

44. Ibid., 417.

45. Ibid.

46. Ibid.
47. Heller, *Chemical Warfare*, 38–39.
48. "Report to the Secretary of the Interior on the Research Work of the Bureau of Mines on War Gas Investigations, July 1, 1917 to May 15, 1918," folder 1, box 110, entry 46, War Gas Investigations, RG 70.
49. Ibid.
50. Fries, "Gas in Attack," [December 11, 1919] 7.
51. Vilensky and Sinish, "Blisters as Weapons of War," 14.
52. U.S. Senate Committee on the Judiciary, *Alleged Dye Monopoly*, 694.
53. Ibid.
54. E. K. Marshall, A. S. Loevenhart, and H. C. Bradley, "Appendix A: Summary of Symposium on Mustard Gas Burns," page 18, folder 1, box 112, entry 46, War Gas Investigations, RG 70.
55. Vilensky and Sinish, "Blisters as Weapons of War," 13.
56. Ibid., 14.
57. "Historical Report . . . February 1, 1917 to March 1, 1918."
58. Ibid.
59. Ibid.
60. Heller, "Perils of Unpreparedness," 19.
61. Ibid., 20.
62. Fries and West, *Chemical Warfare*, 53.
63. Ibid., 56.
64. Ibid., 56–57.

Chapter 2. Battle, 1918

1. Heller, *Chemical Warfare*, 40.
2. Garlock, "Some Interesting Experiences," 2.
3. Foulkes, *Gas!*, 299.
4. U.S. House of Representatives Select Committee on Expenditures in the War Department, *War Expenditures*, p. 1937.
5. Fries and West, *Chemical Warfare*, 88, 111.
6. Jackson Guy Lancaster (AFC 2001/001/24036), Diaries and Journals (MS01), Veterans History Project Collection, American Folklife Center, Library of Congress.
7. "Gas Baseball," *Gas Warfare Bulletin*, issued by the Chief of Engineers, U.S. Army, number 8, May 11, 1918, page 28, box 1727, entry 377, Army School of the Line, A.E.F. General Headquarters, RG 120.
8. "Schedule of Instruction for Students at the Army Gas School, August 19–24, 1918," folder: Schedules, box 1725, entry 377, Army School of the Line, RG 120.
9. "Fourth Corps Replacement Battalion Gas Office; Report for Week ending 2 November, 1918," November 4, 1918, page 1, box 93, entry 915, 2nd Army, Chief of Chem. Warfare, Corresp. by Subject, RG 120.
10. Ibid.
11. "Realistic Training," *Gas Warfare Bulletin*, issued by the Chief of Engineers, U.S. Army, Number 9, July 1, 1918, page 1, box 111, entry 46, War Gas Investigations, RG 70.
12. Fries and West, *Chemical Warfare*, 89.

13. Letter from Captain W. E. Vawter, Gas Officer 33rd Division, to Chief of the Chemical Warfare Service, box 93, entry 915, 2nd Army, Chief of Chem. Warfare, Corresp. by Subject, RG 120.

14. Ibid.

15. Cook, *No Place to Run*, 215.

16. Letter from Captain W. E. Vawter.

17. "Notes on Gas Attacks against American Forces," *Gas Warfare Bulletin*, issued by the Chief of Engineers, U.S. Army, Number 7, May 11, 1918, page 5, box 1727, entry 377, Army School of the Line, RG 120.

18. Fries and West, *Chemical Warfare*, 90.

19. Ibid.

20. Heller, *Chemical Warfare*, 64.

21. "Misuse of the S. B. R.," *Gas Warfare Bulletin*, issued by the Chief of Engineers, U.S. Army, number 12, September 10, 1918, page 2, box 1727, entry 377, Army School of the Line, RG 120.

22. Ibid.

23. Crowell, *America's Munitions*, 428.

24. "Report to the Secretary of the Interior on the Research Work of the Bureau of Mines on War Gas Investigations, July 1, 1917 to May 15, 1918," folder 1, box 110, entry 46, War Gas Investigations, RG 70.

25. Heller, *Chemical Warfare*, 65.

26. E. W. Spencer, "The History of Gas Attacks upon the American Expeditionary Forces During the World War" (typescript, 1928), 500, U.S. Army Heritage and Education Center.

27. Heller, *Chemical Warfare*, 66.

28. Ibid., 65.

29. Crowell, *America's Munitions*, 429.

30. Ibid.

31. Heller, *Chemical Warfare*, 67.

32. U.S. Surgeon General's Office, *Medical Aspects of Gas Warfare*, 61–64.

33. Heller, *Chemical Warfare*, 70–71.

34. "Notes on Gas Attacks," 6.

35. *Gas Warfare: Part II*, 28.

36. Ibid.

37. Ibid.

38. Heller, *Chemical Warfare*, 61.

39. Spencer, "History of Gas Attacks," 1–2.

40. Ibid., 3.

41. Ibid., 6–23; Heller, "Perils of Unpreparedness," 23.

42. Spencer, "History of Gas Attacks," 6.

43. Ibid., 19.

44. Ibid., 19–20.

45. Ibid., 12.

46. Ibid., 11.

47. Cochrane, *Gas Warfare: Study 20*, 65–66.

48. Spencer, "History of Gas Attacks," 131.

49. Hill, "History of the Medical Management," in Tuorinsky, *Medical Aspects*, 93.

50. Ibid., 97–99.
51. Eugene A. Curtin (AFC 2001/001/1379), page 72, Correspondence (MS01), Veterans History Project Collection, American Folklife Center, Library of Congress.
52. *Gas Warfare: Part III*, 48–49; Heller, *Chemical Warfare*, 48.
53. Cochrane, *Gas Warfare: Study 1*, 10.
54. Ibid.
55. Spencer, "History of Gas Attacks," 403.
56. Ibid., 458–59.
57. Ibid., 40–57.
58. Ibid., 54.
59. Addison, *First Gas Regiment*, 44.
60. Ibid., 48–49.
61. Ibid., 51.
62. Cochrane, *Gas Warfare: Study 20*, 25–30.
63. Addison, *First Gas Regiment*, 55–56.
64. Ibid., 55–78, 56.
65. Clark, *Effectiveness of Chemical Weapons*, 10.
66. Prentiss, *Chemicals in War*, 463.
67. "Lecture by Lt-Col Ernest McCullough on the use of Gas in Warfare," box 1725, entry 377, Army School of the Line, RG 120.
68. "Instructions for the Use of Chemical Shells by Artillery" (General Headquarters, American Expeditionary Forces, Office of the Chief of Gas Service, January, 1918), 3–4, U.S. Army Heritage and Education Center.
69. "Lecture by Lt-Col Ernest McCullough."
70. "Instructions," 3.
71. Ibid.
72. Ibid., 6.
73. Fries and West, *Chemical Warfare*, 202.
74. Coffman, *War to End All Wars*, 141–42; Mead, *The Doughboys*, 98.
75. Letter from Franklin K. Lane, U.S. Secretary of the Interior, to Woodrow Wilson, President of the United States, May 15, 1918, folder 1, box 110, entry 46, War Gas Investigations, RG 70.
76. "By Order of the President," 590.
77. "Memorandum Regarding Conference Held in the Office of the Secretary of War, from 3:00 P.M. to 4:45 P.M., May 25, 1918, Regarding the Proposed Transfer of the War Gas Investigations of the Bureau of Mines to the War Department, Under Major General Sibert, Chief of the Gas Service," folder 1, box 110, entry 46, War Gas Investigations, RG 70.
78. Ibid.
79. Ibid.
80. Ibid.
81. "Cable History of the Subject 'Chemical Warfare Service,'" Cable from Pershing 1240, June 3, 1918, page 1, folder: W. D. Chemical Warfare Service 7–63.1, box 220, entry 310, Records of the Historical Section Relating to the History of the War Department, 1900–41, RG 165.
82. Letter from Newton Baker, Secretary of War, to Woodrow Wilson, President of the United States, June 25, 1918, folder 2, box 110, entry 46, War Gas Investigations, RG 70.

83. Letter from Woodrow Wilson, President of the United States, to Van H. Manning, Director of the Bureau of Mines, June 26, 1918, folder 2, box 110, entry 46, War Gas Investigations, RG 70.

84. Letter from Van H. Manning, Director of the Bureau of Mines, to General William L. Sibert, Director, Gas Service, June 29, 1918, folder 2, box 110, entry 46, War Gas Investigations, RG 70.

85. "Transfer of the Experiment Station," 654; "Chemical Warfare Service: Its History and Personnel," 379–80; "Chemical Warfare Service: National Army," 230.

86. "Government Mobilization of Technical Men," 284.

87. "War Department Discovers the Chemist," 165; "Present Status," 639; "War Service of Chemists," 730.

88. Bogert, "Cooperation," 581.

89. Fries and West, *Chemical Warfare*, 145.

90. Ibid., 133.

91. "United States Chemical Warfare Service—II," 372.

92. *The Edgewood Arsenal, Edgewood Maryland* (published as vol. 1, issue 5 of *Chemical Warfare* [March 1919]), 7–8.

93. "United States Chemical Warfare Service—II," 372.

94. Fries and West, *Chemical Warfare*, 55.

95. "United States Chemical Warfare Service—II," 373.

96. Green, "Chlorine-Caustic Soda Plant," 17.

97. Ibid., 17–24.

98. Faith, "'We Are Still.'"

99. Loach, "Mustard Gas Production," 10; Fries and West, *Chemical Warfare*, 155.

100. Loach, "Mustard Gas Production," 11.

101. Ibid.

102. Ibid.

103. Fries and West, *Chemical Warfare*, 153.

104. Loach, "Mustard Gas Production," 11.

105. Ibid., quoting Hanson, 14.

106. Ibid.

107. Ibid., 13.

108. Ibid.

109. Fries and West, *Chemical Warfare*, 59.

110. U.S. Senate Committee on Military Affairs, *Reorganization of the Army*, part 6, 321.

111. Loach, "Mustard Gas Production," 12.

112. Ibid., 13.

113. U.S. House of Representatives Select Committee on Expenditures in the War Department, *War Expenditures*, p. 1944.

114. Ibid.

115. Spencer, "History of Gas Attacks," 211–14.

116. Addison, *First Gas Regiment*, 65–68.

117. J. D. Law, 2nd Lieutenant, Chemical Warfare Service, "Orders No. 60," August 30, 1918, folder: S.O. #(12a–20a) 1918, Hdq. A.E.F., 1st Gas Reg., box 85, entry 1248, Chemical Warfare Service, World War I Organization Records, RG 120.

118. Ibid.
119. Addison, *First Gas Regiment*, 84–92.
120. Ibid., 89.
121. Ibid., 92.
122. Ibid., 113.
123. Ibid., 102.
124. Spencer, "History of Gas Attacks," 523.
125. Ibid.
126. Ibid., 553.
127. Mead, *Doughboys*, 284–99.
128. Addison, *First Gas Regiment*, 115–16.
129. Ibid., 120.
130. Ibid., 119–23.
131. Cochrane, *Gas Warfare: Study 5*, 1.
132. Addison, *First Gas Regiment*, 126.
133. Ibid.
134. Lengel, *To Conquer Hell*, quoting Major Jennings Wise, 391.
135. Cochrane, *Gas Warfare: Study 8*, 1.
136. Mead, *Doughboys*, 299–330.
137. Addison, *First Gas Regiment*, 133–47.
138. Ibid., 146.
139. Spencer, "History of Gas Attacks," 401.
140. Addison, *First Gas Regiment*, 207.
141. Prentiss, *Chemicals in War*, 684.
142. Fries, "Gas in Attack," [December 11, 1919] 4–5.
143. Fries, "Gas in Attack," [December 25, 1919] 2; Harbord, *American Army in France*, 223; Price, *Chemical Weapons Taboo*, 61–62.
144. Fries, "Raining Molten Metal," 15.
145. Vilensky, *Dew of Death*, 1–55; Vilensky and Sinish, "Blisters as Weapons of War," 12–17.
146. Vilensky, *Dew of Death*, 51–54.
147. Ibid., 50–72.
148. Haber, *Poisonous Cloud*, quoting a CWS circular July 11, 1918, 224.
149. Haber concluded that "the CWS was seen by its protagonists as a turning-point in the history of warfare. In practice it was nothing of the kind. The new branch made no significant contribution to the American military potential." Haber, *Poisonous Cloud*, 143.

Chapter 3. Crisis, 1919–1920

1. *Army Almanac*, 692–93.
2. "Present Strength," 610; "Fries Made a Brigadier General," 92.
3. "Chemical Warfare Service Appropriation Urged," 1189.
4. Price, *Chemical Weapons Taboo*, 18.
5. Ibid., 58.
6. U.S. Surgeon General's Office, *Medical Department: Medical Aspects*, 274; Prentiss, *Chemicals in War*, 671.

Notes to Chapter 3

7. "Women's Parade and Governor Cox's Speech Stir the Loyal People of the Community to White Heat of Patriotism," *Portsmouth Daily Times*, June 21, 1918.
8. Haldane, *Callinicus*, 1.
9. Cornwell, *Hitler's Scientists*, 67–68.
10. Slotten, "Humane Chemistry," 476–98.
11. Irwin, *Next War*.
12. Pultz, *Preaching Ministry*, 180.
13. Clarke, *Voices Prophesying War*, 131.
14. March, *Nation at War*, 333.
15. Ibid.
16. Ibid., 333–36.
17. Pershing, *Final Report*, 76–77.
18. U.S. House of Representatives and U.S. Senate Committees on Military Affairs, *Army Reorganization*, 1507–8.
19. Letter from Amos A. Fries, Colonel, Assistant to the Director of the Chemical Warfare Service, to E. J. Atkisson, Lt. Col, Corps of Engineers Camp Benning Georgia, September 5, 1919, folder: Atkisson—Col. E. J., box 15, entry 7, General Fries' file 1918–1920, A–C, Chemical Warfare Service, Edgewood Arsenal 1917–43, RG 175.
20. "Colonel Walker," 2.
21. Fries, "Sixteen Reasons," 3.
22. "Brigadier General Amos A. Fries," 3–8.
23. Ibid.
24. U.S. House of Representatives Select Committee on Expenditures in the War Department, *War Expenditures*, p. 1932.
25. "Brigadier General Amos A. Fries," 3–8.
26. Letter from Amos A. Fries, Colonel, Chief of the Chemical Warfare Service, to Richmond Mayo-Smith, The Plimpton Press, Norwood, MA, September 25, 1919, folder: Mayo-Smith—Lt. Col. Richmond, box 18, entry 7, General Fries' file 1918–1920, L–O, Chemical Warfare Service, Edgewood Arsenal 1917–43, RG 175.
27. "Scrapping War Chemicals," 97–98.
28. Ibid., 98.
29. Letter from Captain J. Allan Sampson to Major C. M. Mackall, CWS, January 21, 1919, box 93, entry 915, 2nd army, Chief of Chem. Warfare, Corresp. by Subject, RG 120.
30. Letter from Amos A. Fries, Colonel, Chief of the Chemical Warfare Service, to E. J. Atkisson, Lt. Col, Corps of Engineers Camp Benning Georgia, September 5, 1919, folder: Atkisson—Col. E. J., box 15, entry 7, General Fries' file 1918–1920, A–C, Chemical Warfare Service, Edgewood Arsenal 1917–43, RG 175.
31. Ibid.
32. Ibid.
33. Brown, *Chemical Warfare*, 76–77.
34. Letter from Amos A. Fries, Colonel, Chief of the Chemical Warfare Service, to William McPherson, Ohio State University, Columbus, Ohio, July 12, 1919, folder: McPherson—Col. Wm., box 18, entry 7, General Fries' file 1918–1920, L–O, Chemical Warfare Service, Edgewood Arsenal 1917–43, RG 175.
35. Crossett, "Relations Section," 613.

Notes to Chapter 3

36. "Former Chemical Warfare Service Officers Who Are Chemists," September 19, 1919, folder: Fries—Col. (Special Papers–Personal), box 19, entry 7, General Fries' file 1918–1920, O–S, Chemical Warfare Service, Edgewood Arsenal 1917–43, RG 175.

37. Letter from E. N. Johnston, Colonel, Lakehurst Proving Ground, to Amos A. Fries, Colonel, Chief of the Chemical Warfare Service, September 4, 1919, folder: Johnston—Col. E. N., box 17, entry 7, General Fries' file 1918–1920, E–L, Chemical Warfare Service, Edgewood Arsenal 1917–43, RG 175.

38. Letter from Amos A. Fries, Colonel, Chief of the Chemical Warfare Service, to E. N. Johnston, Colonel, Lakehurst Proving Ground, September 11, 1919, folder: Johnston—Col. E.N., box 17, entry 7, General Fries' file 1918–1920, E–L, Chemical Warfare Service, Edgewood Arsenal 1917–43, RG 175.

39. Letter from Amos A. Fries, Colonel, Chief of the Chemical Warfare Service, to H. Z. Osborne Jr., Chief Engineer, Board of Public Utilities, City of Los Angeles, August 7, 1919, folder: Osborne—R.G., box 19, entry 7, General Fries' file 1918–1920, O–S, Chemical Warfare Service, Edgewood Arsenal 1917–43, RG 175.

40. Letter from Amos A. Fries, Colonel, Chief of the Chemical Warfare Service, to Charles E. Richardson, International Coal Products Corporation, August 16, 1919, folder: Richardson—Maj. C. E., box 19, entry 7, General Fries' file 1918–1920, O–S, Chemical Warfare Service, Edgewood Arsenal 1917–43, RG 175.

41. Letter from Amos A. Fries, Colonel, Chief of the Chemical Warfare Service, to E. J. Atkisson, Lt. Col, Corps of Engineers Camp Benning Georgia, September 25, 1919, folder: Atkisson—Col. E. J., box 15, entry 7, General Fries' file 1918–1920, A–C, Chemical Warfare Service, Edgewood Arsenal 1917–43, RG 175.

42. Ibid.

43. George O. Gillingham, memorandum on Edgewood Arsenal publication, folder: Edgewood Arsenal, box 17, entry 7, General Fries' file 1918–1920, E–L, Chemical Warfare Service, Edgewood Arsenal 1917–43, RG 175.

44. "Readers 'Tenshun.'"

45. George O. Gillingham, "Slogans," folder: Edgewood Arsenal, box 17, entry 7, General Fries' file 1918–1920, E–L, Chemical Warfare Service, Edgewood Arsenal 1917–43, RG 175; None of these slogans ever appeared on the journal's masthead.

46. Fries, "Chemical Warfare Service."

47. Fries, "Humanity of Poison Gas," 1–6.

48. Fries, "Gas in Attack," [November 27, 1919], 6.

49. Fries, "Humanity of Poison Gas," 4.

50. U.S. Surgeon General's Office, *Medical Department: Medical Aspects*, 274.

51. For a description of how casualty statistics were collected during World War I see U.S. Surgeon General's Office, *Medical Department, Statistics*, 1187–96; for an analysis of conflicting gas casualty accounts in various battles, see Cochrane, *Gas Warfare, Studies 1–20*.

52. Hilmas, Smart, and Hill, "History of Chemical Warfare," in Tuorinsky, *Medical Aspects*, 41–42.

53. Amos A. Fries, "Gas Casualties among Germans; Abstract of British Reports for April to December 1917 Inclusive on Effect of British Gas on the Enemy," February 6, 1918, folder: B: Attacks, American and Allied, box 1729, entry 377, Army School of the Line, A.E.F. General Headquarters, RG 120.

Notes to Chapter 3

54. "Gas as a Humane Weapon," *New York Times*, July 30, 1922.
55. "U.S. Army Reserve of Gas Material," 12.
56. Memorandum from Amos A. Fries, Colonel, Chemical Warfare Service, to Executive Officer, Edgewood Arsenal, October 15, 1919, folder: Edgewood Arsenal, box 17, entry 7, General Fries' file 1918–1920, E–L, Chemical Warfare Service, Edgewood Arsenal 1917–43, RG 175.
57. Memorandum from Amos A. Fries, Colonel, Chemical Warfare Service, to Adjutant, Edgewood Arsenal, Chemical Warfare Service, July 7, 1919, folder: Adjutant—E. A., box 15, entry 7, General Fries' file 1918–1920, A–C, Chemical Warfare Service, Edgewood Arsenal 1917–43, RG 175.
58. Memorandum from Amos A. Fries, Colonel, Chemical Warfare Service, to William L. Sibert, Director, Chemical Warfare Service, Washington, D.C., February 26, 1920, folder: Chief, Chemical Warfare Service, box 15, entry 7, General Fries' file 1918–1920, A–C, Chemical Warfare Service, Edgewood Arsenal 1917–43, RG 175.
59. Memorandum from Amos A. Fries, Colonel, Chemical Warfare Service, to William L. Sibert, Director, Chemical Warfare Service, Washington, D.C., July 29, 1919, folder: Chief, Chemical Warfare Service, box 15, entry 7, General Fries' file 1918–1920, A–C, Chemical Warfare Service, Edgewood Arsenal 1917–43, RG 175.
60. *Statistical Abstracts*, 232.
61. "War Department Deserts," 165.
62. "Philadelphia Meeting," 279.
63. "Chemical Warfare Service," [September 1919], 199.
64. Reed, *Crusading for Chemistry*, 146.
65. Letter from G. Sevier, Colonel, U.S. Army Engineering and Standardization Branch, to W. W. Parker, Major, Chemical Warfare Service, Washington, D.C., May 20, 1919, folder: E&S Branch—P.S&T Division, box 16, entry 7, General Fries' file 1918–1920, C–E, Chemical Warfare Service, Edgewood Arsenal 1917–43, RG 175.
66. Letter from Amos A. Fries, Chief, Chemical Warfare Service, Washington, D.C., to Commanding Officer, Edgewood Arsenal, May 21, 1920, folder: Chief, Chemical Warfare Service, box 15, entry 7, General Fries' file 1918–1920, A–C, Chemical Warfare Service, Edgewood Arsenal 1917–43, RG 175.
67. Letter from Amos A. Fries, Colonel, Edgewood Arsenal, to Director, Chemical Warfare Service, Washington, D.C., July 10, 1919, folder: Chief, Chemical Warfare Service, box 15, entry 7, General Fries' file 1918–1920, A–C, Chemical Warfare Service, Edgewood Arsenal 1917–43, RG 175.
68. Ibid.
69. Letter from Amos A. Fries, Colonel, Chief of the Chemical Warfare Service, to Gilbert N. Lewis, University of California, Berkley, September 23, 1919, folder: Lewis—Col G. N., box 17, entry 7, General Fries' file 1918–1920, E–L, Chemical Warfare Service, Edgewood Arsenal 1917–43, RG 175.
70. U.S. Senate Committee on Military Affairs, *Reorganization of the Army*, August 8, 1919, part 2, 93.
71. Ibid., 94.
72. Ibid., 95; Senator Scott and his family were on the porch of their home when the cloud surrounded them. Afterward he told the *Washington Post* that the gas "attacked my throat and eyes and blistered my face. It had an acrid smell which

might be said to resemble mustard. We got into the house but it was a narrow escape." "N. B. Scott 'Gassed,'" *Washington Post,* August 4, 1918.

73. U.S. Senate Committee on Military Affairs, *Reorganization of the Army,* August 14, 1919, part 3, 127.

74. Ibid., 136.

75. U.S. Senate Committee on Military Affairs, *Reorganization of the Army,* August 18, 1919, part 4, 178.

76. U.S. Senate Committee on Military Affairs, *Reorganization of the Army,* August 25, 1919, part 6, 317.

77. Ibid.

78. Ibid.

79. Ibid.

80. Ibid., 356–57.

81. Ibid., 359.

82. U.S. Senate Committee on Military Affairs, *Reorganization of the Army,* August 26, 1919, part 7, 410–11.

83. Ibid., 414.

84. Ibid., 416.

85. U.S. Senate Committee on Military Affairs, *Reorganization of the Army,* August 29, 1919, part 9, 502.

86. Ibid., 502–3.

87. Ibid., 504.

88. Ibid., 507–9.

89. "Army Reorganization Act," 2.

90. Letter from George E. Chamberlain, Senator, Washington, D.C., to Amos A. Fries, Colonel, Chief of the Chemical Warfare Service, September 19, 1919, folder: Chamberlain—Sen. Geo. E, box 15, entry 7, General Fries' file 1918–1920, A–C, Chemical Warfare Service, Edgewood Arsenal 1917–43, RG 175.

91. Ibid.

92. Letter from Amos A. Fries, Colonel, Chief of the Chemical Warfare Service, to George E. Chamberlain, Senator, Washington, D.C., August 20, 1919, folder: Chamberlain—Sen. Geo. E, box 15, entry 7, General Fries' file 1918–1920, A–C, Chemical Warfare Service, Edgewood Arsenal 1917–43, RG 175.

93. "General Sibert," 755.

94. "Colonel Fries Heads Chemical Warfare Service," 1.

Chapter 4. Improvement, 1921–1925

1. Coffman, *Regulars,* 233.

2. Memorandum from B. H. Wells, Chemical Warfare Service, to Army Chief of Staff, October 10, 1921, folder 381-1-28, box 18, entry 4, Secret and Confidential Files, Central Correspondence, 1918–1942, Records of the Office of the Chief, RG 175.

3. Kreidberg and Henry, *History of Military Mobilization;* for the early 1920s, see 377–416.

4. Memorandum from Amos A. Fries, General, Chief of the Chemical Warfare Service, to the Adjutant General, October 30, 1924, folder 381-29-90, box 19, entry 4, Secret and Confidential Files, Records of the Office of the Chief, RG 175.

Notes to Chapter 4

5. "Warning! Beware the Gas-Mask!," 305–6.
6. Fieldner and Katz, "Use of Army Gas Masks," 582.
7. Ibid.
8. "Industrial Gas Mask," 125.
9. "Universal Gas Mask," 982.
10. Memorandum from John W. Weeks, Secretary of War, to Commanding Generals of all Corps Areas, the Chiefs of all War Department Branches, the Chief of the Militia Bureau and the Commanding General, District of Washington, June 10, 1924, folder 381–48, box 18, entry 4, Secret and Confidential Files, Records of the Office of the Chief, RG 175; Millett and Maslowski, *For the Common Defense*, 377–78.
11. Memorandum from Amos A. Fries, General, Chief of the Chemical Warfare Service, to All Chemical Warfare Reserve Officers, July 12, 1924, folder 381–48, box 18, entry 4, Secret and Confidential Files, Records of the Office of the Chief, RG 175.
12. Memorandum from Major William N. Porter, to Major Frazer, Office of the Assistant Chief of Staff, G–4, August 28, 1924, folder 381–48, box 18, entry 4, Secret and Confidential Files, Records of the Office of the Chief, RG 175.
13. Letter form Amos A. Fries General, Chief of the Chemical Warfare Service, to H. A. Drum, Brigadier General, Assistant Chief of Staff, October 15, 1924, folder 322.095–566, box 12, entry 4, Secret and Confidential Files, Records of the Office of the Chief, RG 175.
14. Order from John W. Weeks, Secretary of War, to Commanding Generals of All Corps Areas and the Commanding General, District of Washington, August 21, 1924, folder 381–48, box 18, entry 4, Secret and Confidential Files, Records of the Office of the Chief, RG 175.
15. Memorandum from Amos A. Fries, General, Chief of the Chemical Warfare Service, to Assistant Secretary of War, Washington, D.C., Attn: Director of Procurement, September 5, 1924, folder 381–48, box 18, entry 4, Secret and Confidential Files, Records of the Office of the Chief, RG 175.
16. Memorandum from Amos A. Fries, General, Chief of the Chemical Warfare Service, to the Adjutant General, Washington, D.C., October 3, 1924, folder 381–49, box 18, entry 4, Secret and Confidential Files, Records of the Office of the Chief, RG 175.
17. Memorandum from Amos A. Fries, General, Chief of the Chemical Warfare Service, to John W. Weeks, Secretary of War, February 18, 1925, folder 470.72–3170–3303, box 38, entry 4, Secret and Confidential Files, Records of the Office of the Chief, RG 175.
18. Ibid.
19. Stockholm International Peace Research Institute, *Problem*, 3:153–54.
20. Report on New Agencies of Warfare, Submitted by the Sub-committee on New Agencies of Warfare and Adopted by the Advisory Committee, December 1, 1921, folder: Report on Poison Gas, box 1, entry 94, Special Reports Prepared by the Advisory Committee 1921–1922, International Conference Records, Conference on the Limitation of Armaments, U.S. Delegation, RG 43.
21. Ibid.
22. Committee on General Information of the Advisory Committee to the American Delegation, Special Bulletin No. 5, January 14, 1922, folder: Commit-

tee on Gen. Info—Special Bulletin #5 January 14, 1922, box 4, entry 93, News Summaries, December 1, 1921–January 28, 1922, Summaries No. 39–50, Foreign Language Newspaper 1921, Periodical Comment, January 16, 1922, International Conference Records, Conference on the Limitation of Armaments, U.S. Delegation, RG 43.

23. Report on New Agencies of Warfare, Submitted by the Sub-committee on New Agencies of Warfare and Adopted by the Advisory Committee, December 1, 1921, folder: Report on Poison Gas, box 1, entry 94, Special Reports Prepared by the Advisory Committee 1921–1922, International Conference Records, Conference on the Limitation of Armaments, U.S. Delegation, RG 43.

24. Memorandum from Amos A. Fries, Chief, Chemical Warfare Service, to the Assistant Chief of Staff, War Plans Division, General Staff, October 17, 1921, page 6, folder 1, box 1, entry 4, Secret and Confidential Files, Records of the Office of the Chief, RG 175.

25. Ibid., 4.

26. Reed, *Crusading for Chemistry*, 150–55.

27. Stockholm International Peace Research Institute, *Problem*, 3:22.

28. Miller, *War Plan Orange*; Ross, *American War Plans: 1919–1941*, 5 vols.; Ross, *American War Plans: 1890–1939*.

29. For selections from Plan Green see Ross, *American War Plans: 1919–1941*, vol. 1.

30. "Major General Sibert," 3.

31. Ibid.

32. Memorandum from Amos A. Fries, General, Chief of the Chemical Warfare Service, to the Assistant Chief of Staff, War Plans Division, November 29, 1922, folder 381/1–25, box 17, entry 4, Secret and Confidential Files, Records of the Office of the Chief, RG 175.

33. Ibid.

34. Ibid.

35. Letter from H. H. Tebbetts, Adjutant General, to Commanding General 8th Corps Area, Fort Sam Huston, TX, December 5, 1922, folder 381/1–25, box 17, entry 4, Secret and Confidential Files, Records of the Office of the Chief, RG 175.

36. Ibid.

37. Memorandum from George M. Russell, A.C. of S., G–2, to Chief of Staff, Eighth Corps Area, November 2, 1922, folder 400.112–87–110, box 26, entry 4, Secret and Confidential Files, Records of the Office of the Chief, RG 175.

38. Letter from George A. MacKay, Chemical Warfare Officer, Ft. Houston, TX, to Amos A. Fries, General, Chief of the Chemical Warfare Service, November 1, 1922, folder 400.112–87–110, box 26, entry 4, Secret and Confidential Files, RG 175.

39. Ibid.

40. Ibid.

41. Ibid.

42. Farwell, "Monthly Review," 174.

43. Letter from William N. Porter, Major, Chemical Warfare Service, Assistant Executive Officer, to George M. Halloran, Major, Chemical Warfare Service, Headquarters of the 8th Corps Area, Ft. Houston, Texas, December 19, 1924, folder

381–29–90, box 19, entry 4, Secret and Confidential Files, Records of the Office of the Chief, RG 175.

44. Letter from George M. Halloran, Major, Chemical Warfare Service, Headquarters of the 8th Corps Area, Ft. Houston, Texas, to William N. Porter, Major, Chemical Warfare Service, Assistant Executive Officer, January 19, 1925, folder 381–29–90, box 19, entry 4, Secret and Confidential Files, Records of the Office of the Chief, RG 175.

45. "Lenroot Impressed at Edgewood," 668.
46. "Chemical Exhibit a Success," 1119.
47. "General Fries Announces," 541.
48. American Dyes Institute, *World Disarmament*.
49. "Army's Testimony on Dye Protection," 6.
50. Fries, "Chemical Warfare and the Chemical Profession," 3.
51. Ibid.
52. "Dupont Officials Deny Any Threat Whatever; Nation Needs Dye Plants," *Washington Post*, (May 8, 1920).
53. U.S. Senate Committee on the Judiciary, *Alleged Dye Monopoly*.
54. "Farewell to the Dye Investigation."
55. "Gas as a Humane Weapon," *New York Times*, July 30, 1922.
56. Fries, "Gas in Attack," [November 27, 1919], 7.
57. "Alleged Gas Injuries," 543.
58. U.S. War Department, *Report*, 281.
59. Ibid.
60. Ibid., 282.
61. More current studies on the long-term effects of chemical weapons exposure are: Carr, Denman, and Skinner, "Noxious Gases and Bronchiectasis;" Freitag et al., "Role of Bronchoscopy;" Emad and Rezaian, "Diversity;" Ghanei et al., "Tracheobronchomalacia."
62. Whittemore, "World War I."
63. Hale, "Introduction," in Yerkes, *New World of Science*, viii.
64. "Chemical Warfare," [January 1922], 32.
65. In her book on the British war gas program in World War I, Marion Girard found that the "controlled approaches" of the members of the scientific community "discouraged emotional reactions to gas and helpless feelings about it," and that "in addition, their constant interactions with gas further desensitized them to its novelty and the barbarity perceived by others." Girard, *Strange and Formidable Weapon*, 76.
66. See *Chemical Age* issues 31, no. 3 (March 1923) to 31, no. 11 (November 1923).
67. Memorandum from E. J. Atkisson, Major, Chemical Warfare Service, to Commanding Officer, Edgewood Arsenal, October 17, 1921, folder 400.112–87–110, box 26, entry 4, Secret and Confidential Files, Records of the Office of the Chief, RG 175.
68. "Project Program Chemical Warfare Service and Ordinance Department," folder 400.112–87–110, box 26, entry 4, Secret and Confidential Files, Records of the Office of the Chief, RG 175.
69. Ibid.
70. Waller, *Question of Loyalty*, 169.

71. Farrow, *Gas Warfare*, vii.

72. Waller, *Question of Loyalty*; Jeffers, *Billy Mitchell*.

73. Hone and Hone, *Battle Line*, 90–109.

74. Photos of the test were later published in "Chemical Warfare in Naval Action," 498–99.

75. Letter from Amos A. Fries, General, Chief of the Chemical Warfare Service, to Major J. W. N. Schulz, General Service Schools, Ft. Leavenworth, Kansas, November 28, 1921, folder 381-1-28, box 18, entry 4, Secret and Confidential Files, Records of the Office of the Chief, RG 175.

76. "Naval Influence in Abolishing Chemical Warfare," 1.

77. Ibid.

78. "Airplanes Make Fog, Hiding Operations," *New York Times*, June 3, 1923.

79. Ibid.

80. Waller, *Question of Loyalty*, 1–62.

81. Ibid, 169–71.

82. Folder 381-1-28, box 18, entry 4, Secret and Confidential Files, Records of the Office of the Chief, RG 175.

83. "Chemical Warfare Making Swords into Plowshares," 3.

84. "War on Rats," 543.

85. "Department of Agriculture," 543.

86. "Chemical Warfare Gas," 39; Fries, "By-Products," 1079–84.

87. "Edison's Suggestion to Use Poison Gas in Trapping Animals Taken Up by Army," *New York Times*, November 23, 1923.

88. Fries and West, *Chemical Warfare*, 430.

89. Russell, *War and Nature*.

90. "Mustard Gas Drives Off Safe Robbers Who Blew Open a Michigan Bank Vault," *New York Times*, February 16, 1921.

91. Letter from Amos A. Fries, General, Chief of the Chemical Warfare Service, to E. J. Atkisson, Major, Chemical Warfare Service, June 30, 1921, folder 470.61, box 35, entry 4, Secret and Confidential Files, Records of the Office of the Chief, RG 175.

92. Ibid.

93. Ibid.

94. Letter from R. Simmons, Chief Inspector, Post Office Department, to A. Gibson, Major, Chemical Warfare Service, September 8, 1921, folder 470.61, box 35, entry 4, Secret and Confidential Files, Records of the Office of the Chief, RG 175.

95. "War Gas Routs Yeggmen," *Los Angeles Times*, July 10, 1925.

96. Vedder and Sawyer, "Chlorine as a Therapeutic Agent," 764–66.

97. Vedder, "Present Status," 21–29.

98. Vedder, *Medical Aspects*, xii.

99. "Army's Chlorine Gas Helps Coolidge's Cold: He Spends 45 Minutes in Air-Tight Room," *New York Times*, May 21, 1924.

100. "Gas Treatment Taken Again By Coolidge," *New York Times*, May 22, 1924.

101. "Coolidge's Cold is Cured," *New York Times*, May 24, 1924.

102. "Gen. Fries Defends Chlorine Treatment," *New York Times*, January 6, 1925.

103. Ibid.
104. Diehl, "Value of Chlorine," 1629–32.
105. Laurie and Cole, *Role of Federal Military*, 357.
106. Ibid.
107. Letter from A. C. Dillingham, Director of Public Safety, Norfolk, VA, to Amos A. Fries, Colonel, Chief of the Chemical Warfare Service, September 19, 1919, folder: Dillingham—Rear Admiral A. C., box 16, entry 7, General Fries' file 1918–1920, C–E, Chemical Warfare Service, Edgewood Arsenal 1917–43, RG 175.
108. Ibid.
109. Letter from Amos A. Fries, Colonel, Chief of the Chemical Warfare Service, to A. C. Dillingham, Director of Public Safety, Norfolk, VA, December 10, 1919, Folder: Dillingham—Rear Admiral A. C., box 16, entry 7, General Fries' file 1918–1920, C–E, Chemical Warfare Service, Edgewood Arsenal 1917–43, RG 175.
110. Letter from Amos A. Fries, General, Chief of the Chemical Warfare Service, to Major J. W. N. Schulz, General Service Schools, Ft. Leavenworth, Kansas, November 28, 1921, folder 381-1-28, box 18, entry 4, Secret and Confidential Files, Records of the Office of the Chief, RG 175.
111. "Girl Scouts Weep in Tear-Gas Visit," *Washington Post*, August 7, 1921.
112. Ibid.
113. Laurie and Cole, *Role of Federal Military*, 358.
114. Ibid., 322.
115. Ibid., 360.
116. Ibid., 358–61.
117. Banner, *Death Penalty*, 196–97.
118. *State v. Gee Jon*, 46 Nev. 418, 211 P. 676 (1923).
119. Laurie and Cole, *Role of Federal Military*, 256.
120. Hapgood, *Professional Patriots*, 168.
121. Fries, *Communism Unmasked*, 15.
122. Ibid.
123. Murphy, *Meaning of the Freedom of Speech*, 191–98; Jensen, "All Pink Sisters," in Scharf and Jensen, *Decades of Discontent*; Lemons, *Woman Citizen*, 209–27; Nielsen, *Un-American Womanhood*, 73–88.
124. Maxwell, "The Socialist-Pacifist Movement in America is an Absolutely Fundamental and Integral Part of International Socialism," *Dearborn Independent*, March 22, 1924.
125. Jensen, "All Pink Sisters," 212.
126. Murphy, *Meaning of the Freedom of Speech*, 191.
127. One historian of the feminist movement, J. Stanley Lemons, concluded that "while social feminism faced a number of difficulties in the late 1920s, one of the most emotion-charged and persistent problems was its entanglement in the spider web controversy"; Lemons, *Woman Citizen*, 225.
128. E. J. Atkisson, Major, Chemical Warfare Service, "Report on Chemical Warfare in Connection with the Conference for the Control of the International Trade in Arms, Munitions and Implements of War. Geneva, Switzerland, May–June, 1925," page 1, folder 319.1-1997, box 9, entry 4, Secret and Confidential Files, Records of the Office of the Chief, RG 175.
129. Ibid., 2.
130. Stockholm International Peace Research Institute, *Problem*, 3:155.

131. Fujitani, "United States and Chemical Warfare," 62–84; Brown, *Chemical Warfare*, 98–110.

132. E. J. Atkisson, Major, Chemical Warfare Service, "Report on Chemical Warfare in Connection with the Conference for the Control of the International Trade in Arms, Munitions and Implements of War. Geneva, Switzerland, May–June, 1925," page 2, folder 319.1-1997, box 9, entry 4, Secret and Confidential Files, Records of the Office of the Chief, RG 175.

133. Ibid., 14.

134. Ibid., 19.

135. Fujitani, "United States and Chemical Warfare," 82.

136. E. P. H. Gempel, Captain, Philippine Department, Chemical Warfare Service, "The Protection of the Coast Defenses of Manila & Subic Bay Against Gas," October 1, 1925, folder 354.2/1–8, box 15, entry 4, Secret and Confidential Files, Records of the Office of the Chief, RG 175.

137. Ibid.

Chapter 5. Legacy, 1926–1929

1. Fujitani, "United States and Chemical Warfare," 91.
2. *Congressional Record*, 69th Congress 2nd Session, December 9, 1926, 144.
3. Ibid., 146.
4. Ibid.
5. Ibid.
6. Ibid.
7. Ibid., 153–54.
8. *Congressional Record*, 69th Congress 2nd Session, January 19, 1927, 1969; Brown, *Chemical Warfare*, 103–104n9.
9. *Congressional Record*, 69th Congress 2nd Session, January 19, 1927, 1969.
10. *Congressional Record*, 69th Congress 2nd Session, December 10, 1926, 226.
11. *Congressional Record*, 69th Congress 2nd Session, December 13, 1926, 367.
12. Ibid.
13. Ibid., 368.
14. Ibid.; Fujitani, "United States and Chemical Warfare," 104.
15. Adelno Gibson, "The U.S. Policy with Respect to Chemical Warfare and the Training Policy Thereunder: Lecture" (typescript, 1933), 6, U.S. Army Heritage and Education Center.
16. Ibid., 7.
17. Folder 354.2/1–8, box 15, entry 4, Secret and Confidential Files, Central Correspondence, 1918-1942, Records of the Office of the Chief, RG 175.
18. Ibid.
19. "Proceedings of the Coast Artillery Board; Project No. 566-D," January 9, 1932, folder 660.2, box 40, entry 4, Secret and Confidential Files, Records of the Office of the Chief, RG 175.
20. Memorandum from C. E. Brigham, Lieut. Col., Executive Officer, Chemical Warfare Service, to Chief, Bureau of Aeronautics, Navy Department, November 28, 1927, folder 400.112/1–8, box 25, entry 4, Secret and Confidential Files, Records of the Office of the Chief, RG 175.

Notes to Chapter 5

21. Memorandum from B. M. Thompson, Lieutenant Commander, USN, Naval War College, March 8, 1928, folder 727, box 45, entry 4, Secret and Confidential Files, Records of the Office of the Chief, RG 175.

22. *Exhibit of the Chemical Warfare Service.*

23. Ibid., 8.

24. Prentiss, *Chemicals in War*, 247.

25. Folder 354.2–3, box 15, entry 4, Secret and Confidential Files, Records of the Office of the Chief, RG 175.

26. Folder 111/26–36, box 2, entry 4, Secret and Confidential Files, Records of the Office of the Chief, RG 175.

27. Amos A. Fries, General, Chief of the Chemical Warfare Service, to the Adjutant General, October 14, 1926, folder 470.72–3170–3303, box 38, entry 4, Secret and Confidential Files, Records of the Office of the Chief, RG 175.

28. Ibid.

29. Memorandum from A. M. Hermitage, Major, Chemical Warfare Service, to Amos A. Fries, General, Chief of the Chemical Warfare Service, Washington, D.C., April 1, 1927, folder 470.72–3170–3303, box 38, entry 4, Secret and Confidential Files, Records of the Office of the Chief, RG 175.

30. Ibid.

31. Ibid.

32. Order from Dwight F. Davis, Secretary of War, to Amos A. Fries, General, Chief of the Chemical Warfare Service, November 23, 1928, folder 381.4–30–50, box 22, entry 4, Secret and Confidential Files, Records of the Office of the Chief, RG 175.

33. "Major-General Gilchrist Heads C.W.S.," 259; Fries was succeeded by Harry L. Gilchrist, an officer formerly of the Army Medical Corps who had served with the CWS for the previous ten years.

34. Koistinen, *Military-Industrial Complex*; Brandes, *Warhogs*; Feaver and Kohn, *Soldiers and Civilians.*

35. Price, *Chemical Weapons Taboo*, 73.

36. Brown, *Chemical Warfare*, 110–21.

37. Hilmas, Smart, and Hill, "History of Chemical Warfare," in Tuorinsky, *Medical Aspects*, 48.

38. Rosenman, *Public Papers and Addresses of Franklin D. Roosevelt*, 242.

39. Ibid., 243.

40. Hilmas, Smart, and Hill, "History of Chemical Warfare," in Tuorinsky, *Medical Aspects*, 48–50.

41. Duffy, *Nuclear Politics in America*, 31.

42. Ibid., 33.

43. Hilmas, Smart, and Hill, "History of Chemical Warfare," in Tuorinsky, *Medical Aspects*, 57.

44. Mauroni, *America's Struggle*, 50.

45. Mauroni, "U.S. Army Chemical Corps;" Hilmas, Smart, and Hill, "History of Chemical Warfare," 59–61.

46. Mauroni, *America's Struggle*, 146.

47. Mauroni, *Chemical Demilitarization.*

48. Fries, "Chemical Warfare—Past and Future," 4.

BIBLIOGRAPHY

Archival Materials

Unless otherwise indicated, all archival material came from the U.S. National Archives in College Park, Maryland, from Record Group 43, Records of International Conferences, Commissions and Expositions; Record Group 70, Records of the U.S. Bureau of Mines; Record Group 120, Records of the American Expeditionary Forces (World War I); Record Group 165, Records of the War Department General and Special Staffs; and Record Group 175, Records of the Chemical Warfare Service.

Published Sources

Addison, James Thayer. *The Story of the First Gas Regiment*. Boston: Houghton Mifflin, 1919.
"Alleged Gas Injuries Being Investigated." *Chemical and Metallurgical Engineering* 24, no. 8 (February 23, 1921): 543.
American Battle Monuments Commission. *American Armies and Battlefields in Europe: A History, Guide, and Reference Book*. Washington: U.S. GPO, 1938.
American Dyes Institute. *World Disarmament and the Master Key Industry*. New York: American Dyes Institute, 1921.
The Army Almanac. Washington: U.S. GPO, 1950.
"Army Reorganization Act." *Chemical Warfare* 4, no. 4 (June 10, 1920): 2.
"The Army's Testimony on Dye Protection." *American Dyestuff Reporter* 9, no. 18 (October 31, 1921): 6.
Banner, Stuart. *The Death Penalty: An American History*. Cambridge: Harvard University Press, 2002.
Bogert, Marston T. "Cooperation of the American Chemical Society with the Chemical Service Section." *Journal of Industrial and Engineering Chemistry* 10, no. 7 (July 1918): 581.
Brandes, Stuart D. *Warhogs: A History of War Profits in America*. Lexington: University Press of Kentucky, 1997.
"Brigadier General Amos A. Fries." *Chemical Warfare* 3, no. 2 (February 26, 1920): 3–8.
Brophy, Leo P., and George J. B. Fisher. *The Chemical Warfare Service: Organizing for War*. Washington: U.S. GPO, 1989.
Brophy, Leo P., Wyndham D. Miles, and Rexmond C. Cochrane. *The Chemical Warfare Service: From Laboratory to Field*. Washington: U.S. GPO, 1988.

Brown, Frederick J. *Chemical Warfare: A Study in Restraints*. New Brunswick, N.J.: Transaction, 2006.

Bruce, Robert V. *Lincoln and the Tools of War*. Chicago: University of Illinois Press, 1989.

Burrell, George A. "The Research Division, Chemical Warfare Service, U.S.A." *Journal of Industrial and Engineering Chemistry* 11, no. 2 (February 1919): 93–104.

"By Order of the President." *Journal of Industrial and Engineering Chemistry* 10, no. 8 (August 1918): 590.

Byrd, Kai, and Martin J. Sherwin. *American Prometheus: The Triumph and Tragedy of Robert J. Oppenheimer*. New York: Knopf, 2006.

Carr, Duane, W. E. Denman, and E. F. Skinner. "Noxious Gases and Bronchiectasis." *Chest* 13 (1947): 596–601.

Chambers, John Whiteclay. *The Eagle and the Dove: The American Peace Movement and United States Foreign Policy 1900–1922*. Syracuse: Syracuse University Press, 1991.

"Chemical Exhibit a Success." *Chemical and Metallurgical Engineering* 24, no. 25 (June 22, 1921): 1119.

"Chemical Warfare." *Chemical Age* 30, no. 1 (January 1922): 32.

"Chemical Warfare Gas Used as Fumigant." *Chemical and Metallurgical Engineering* 27, no. 1 (July 5, 1922): 39.

"Chemical Warfare Making Swords into Plowshares." *Chemical Warfare* 8, no. 2 (1922): 2–5.

"Chemical Warfare in Naval Action." *Chemical and Metallurgical Engineering* 26, no. 11 (March 15, 1922): 498–99.

"[The] Chemical Warfare Service." *Chemical Engineer* 27, no. 9 (September 1919): 199.

"[The] Chemical Warfare Service." *Chemical Warfare* 1, no. 9 (October 16, 1919): 4–5.

"Chemical Warfare Service Appropriation Urged on Basis of Research Need." *Chemical and Metallurgical Engineering* 26, no. 25 (June 21, 1922): 1189.

"Chemical Warfare Service: Its History and Personnel." *Chemical Engineer* 26, no. 8 (July 1918): 379–80.

"Chemical Warfare Service: National Army." *Chemical and Metallurgical Engineering* 19, no. 5 (September 1, 1918): 230.

Chickering, Roger, and Stig Forster. *Great War, Total War: Combat and Mobilization on the Western Front, 1914–1918*. Cambridge: Cambridge University Press, 2000.

Clark, Dorothy Kneeland. *Effectiveness of Chemical Weapons in WWI*. Bethesda: Operations Research, Johns Hopkins University, 1959.

Clarke, I. F. *Voices Prophesying War: Future Wars 1763–3749*. Oxford: Oxford University Press, 1992.

Cochrane, Rexmond C. *Gas Warfare in World War I: Study 1; Gas Warfare at Belleau Wood, June 1918*. Army Chemical Center, Md.: U.S. Army Chemical Corps Historical Office, 1957.

———. *Gas Warfare in World War I: Study 5; The Use of Gas at Saint Mihiel; 90th Division, September 1918*. Army Chemical Center, Md.: U.S. Army Chemical Corps Historical Office, 1957.

---. *Gas Warfare in World War I: Study 8; The 33rd Division along the Meuse, October 1918.* Army Chemical Center, Md.: U.S. Army Chemical Corps Historical Office, 1958.

---. *Gas Warfare in World War I: Study 20; The 26th Division East of the Meuse, September 1918.* Army Chemical Center, Md.: U.S. Army Chemical Corps Historical Office, 1960.

Coffman, Edward M. *The Regulars: The American Army; 1898–1941.* Cambridge: Belknap, 2004.

---. *The War to End All Wars: The American Military Experience in World War I.* New York: Oxford University Press, 1968.

"Colonel Fries Heads Chemical Warfare Service." *Chemical and Metallurgical Engineering* 22, no. 9 (March 3, 1920): 1.

"Colonel Walker Gives His Views on Future Activities of C.W.S." *Chemical Warfare* 1, no. 5 (September 18, 1919): 2.

Congressional Record. 69th Congress, 2nd Session.

Conventions and Declarations between the Powers: Concerning War, Arbitration and Neutrality. The Hague: Martinus Nijhoff, 1915.

Cook, Tim. *No Place to Run: The Canadian Corps and Gas Warfare in the First World War.* Vancouver: UBC, 1999.

Cornwell, John. *Hitler's Scientists: Science, War and the Devil's Pact.* New York: Viking Penguin, 2003.

Cott, Nancy F. *The Grounding of Modern Feminism.* New Haven, Conn.: Yale University Press, 1987.

Crossett, Frederick M. "Relations Section, Chemical Warfare Service." *Chemical and Metallurgical Engineering* 21, no. 12 (November 12–19, 1919): 613.

Crowell, Benedict. *America's Munitions: 1917–1918.* Washington: U.S. GPO, 1919.

"Department of Agriculture Criticizes Use of Poison Gas for Boll Weevil Control." *Chemical and Metallurgical Engineering* 24, no. 7 (February 16, 1921): 543.

Diehl, Harold S. "Value of Chlorine in the Treatment of Colds." *Journal of the American Medical Association,* 84 (May 30, 1925): 1629–32.

Duffy, Robert J. *Nuclear Politics in America: A History and Theory of Government Regulation.* Lawrence: University Press of Kansas, 1997.

Eisenhower, John S. D. *Yanks: The Epic Story of the American Army in World War I.* New York: Free Press, 2001.

Emad, A., and G. R. Rezaian. "The Diversity of the Effects of Sulfur Mustard Gas Inhalation on Respiratory System 10 Years after a Single, Heavy Exposure: Analysis of 197 Cases." *Chest* 112 (1997): 734–38.

Exhibit of the Chemical Warfare Service, United States Army. Washington: U.S. GPO, 1927.

Faith, Thomas I. "'As Is Proper in Republican Form of Government': Selling Chemical Warfare to Americans in the 1920s." *Federal History* 2 (January 2010): 28–41.

---. "Under a Green Sea: The U.S. Chemical Warfare Service 1917–1929." Ph.D. diss., George Washington University, 2008.

---. "'We Are Still Letting That Building Alone': The Mustard Gas Plant at Edgewood Arsenal, Maryland, in World War I." *Journal of America's Military Past* 37, no. 3 (Fall 2012): 29–42.

Farrow, Edward S. *Gas Warfare.* New York: Dutton, 1920.
"Farewell to the Dye Investigation." *American Dyestuff Reporter* 10, no. 11 (May 22, 1922): 392–93.
Farwell, Oliver A. "Monthly Review of Botany and Materia Medica." *Bulletin of Pharmacy* 11, no. 4 (April 1897): 173–75.
Feaver, Peter D., and Richard H. Kohn. *Soldiers and Civilians: The Civil-Military Gap and American National Security.* Cambridge, Mass.: MIT Press, 2001.
Fieldner, A. C., and S. H. Katz. "Use of Army Gas Masks in Atmospheres Containing Sulphur Dioxide." *Chemical and Metallurgical Engineering* 20, no. 11 (June 1, 1919): 582.
Foulkes, Charles H., *"Gas!" The Story of the Special Brigade.* Edinburgh: Blackwood, 1934.
Freitag, L. et al. "The Role of Bronchoscopy in Pulmonary Complications due to Mustard Gas Inhalation." *Chest* 100 (1991): 1436–41.
Fries, Amos A. "By-Products of Chemical Warfare." *Industrial and Engineering Chemistry* 20, no. 10 (October 1, 1928): 1079–84.
———. "Chemical Warfare and the Chemical Profession." *Chemical Warfare* 3, no. 12 (May 6, 1920): 3–10.
———. "Chemical Warfare—Past and Future." *Chemical Warfare* 5, no. 1 (July 5, 1920), 4–7.
———. "The Chemical Warfare Service." *Chemical Warfare* 1, no. 1 (August 21, 1919).
———. *Communism Unmasked.* Washington: Georgetown Press, 1937.
———. "Gas in Attack." *Chemical Warfare* 2, no. 2 (November 27, 1919): 2–9.
———. "Gas in Attack." *Chemical Warfare* 2, no. 4 (December 11, 1919): 2–8.
———. "Gas in Attack." *Chemical Warfare* 2, no. 6 (December 25, 1919): 2–8.
———. "The Humanity of Poison Gas." *Chemical Warfare* 1, no. 11 (October 30, 1919): 1–6.
———. "Raining Molten Metal on the Enemy." *Chemical Warfare* 1, no. 9 (October 16, 1919): 15–6.
———. "Sixteen Reasons Why the Chemical Warfare Service Must Be a Separate Department of the Army." *Chemical Warfare* 2, no. 7 (January 1, 1920): 2–4.
Fries, Amos A., and Clarence J. West. *Chemical Warfare.* New York: McGraw Hill, 1921.
"Fries Made a Brigadier General." *Chemical and Metallurgical Engineering* 23, no. 3 (July 21, 1920): 92.
Fujitani, Kevin Takashi. "The United States and Chemical Warfare: The 1925 Geneva Gas Protocol and its Legacy." Master's thesis, University of Hawaii, 1991.
Garlock, J. B. "Some Interesting Experiences with the First Gas Regiment Formerly the 30th Engineers." *Chemical Warfare* 1, no. 13 (November 13, 1919): 2–5.
Gas Warfare: Part II, Method of Defense Against Gas Attacks. Washington: Army War College, January 1918.
Gas Warfare: Part III, Methods of Training in Defensive Measures. Washington: Army War College, January 1918.
"General Fries Announces Policy as to Patents." *Chemical and Metallurgical Engineering* 23, no. 11 (September 15, 1920): 541.
"General Sibert and the Chemical Warfare Service." *Chemical and Metallurgical Engineering* 22, no. 16 (April 21, 1920): 755.

Bibliography

Ghanei, Mostafa, et al. "Tracheobronchomalacia and Air Trapping after Mustard Gas Exposure." *American Journal of Respiratory Critical Care Medicine* 173 (October 27, 2005): 304–9.

Gilchrist, Harry L. *The Residual Effects of Warfare Gasses.* Washington: U.S. GPO, 1933.

Girard, Marion. *A Strange and Formidable Weapon: British Responses to World War I Poison Gas.* Lincoln: University of Nebraska Press, 2008.

Goldhurst, Richard. *Pipe Clay and Drill: John J. Pershing, the Classic American Soldier.* New York: Reader's Digest Press, 1977.

"Government Mobilization of Technical Men." *Chemical Engineer* 26, no. 8 (July 1918): 284.

Green, Samuel M. "The United States Government Chlorine-Caustic Soda Plant at Edgewood Arsenal, Edgewood, Maryland." *Chemical and Metallurgical Engineering* 21, no. 1 (July 1, 1919): 17–24.

Haber, L. F. *The Poisonous Cloud: Chemical Warfare in the First World War.* Oxford: Clarendon, 1986.

Haldane, J. B. S. *Callinicus: A Defense of Chemical Warfare.* New York: Dutton, 1925.

Hapgood, Norman. *Professional Patriots.* New York: Boni, 1927.

Harbord, James G. *The American Army in France 1917–1919.* Boston: Little, Brown, 1936.

Harris, Robert, and Jeremy Paxman. *A Higher Form of Killing: The Secret History of Chemical and Biological Warfare.* New York: Random House, 2002.

Haynes, Williams. *American Chemical Industry.* 6 vols. New York: Garland, 1983.

Heller, Charles E. *Chemical Warfare in World War I: The American Experience, 1917–1918.* Fort Leavenworth, Kan.: U.S. Army Command and General Staff College, 1984.

———. "The Perils of Unpreparedness: The American Expeditionary Forces and Chemical Warfare." *Military Review* 65, no. 1 (January 1985): 12–25.

Hersh, Seymour M. *Chemical and Biological Warfare: America's Hidden Arsenal.* Indianapolis: Bobbs-Merrill, 1968.

Hershberg, James G. *James B. Conant: Harvard to Hiroshima and the Making of the Nuclear Age.* New York: Knopf, 1993.

Hewes, James E. *From Root to McNamara: Army Organization and Administration, 1900–1963.* Washington: U.S. GPO, 1975.

Hone, Thomas C., and Trent Hone. *Battle Line: The United States Navy 1919–1939.* Annapolis: Naval Institute Press, 2006.

"Industrial Gas Mask for Ammonia Approved." *Chemical and Metallurgical Engineering* 25, no. 3 (July 20, 1921): 125.

Irwin, Will. *The Next War: An Appeal to Common Sense.* New York: Dutton, 1921.

Jeffers, H. Paul. *Billy Mitchell: The Life, Times, and Battles of America's Prophet of Air Power.* St. Paul: Zenith, 2005.

Jones, Daniel Patrick. "American Chemists and the Geneva Protocol." *Isis* 71, no. 3 (September 1980): 426–40

———. "The Role of Chemists in Research on War Gases in the United States during World War I." Ph.D. diss., University of Wisconsin, 1969.

Karsten, Peter. *The Military in America: From the Colonial era to the Present.* New York: Free Press, 1980.

Keene, Jennifer D. *Doughboys, the Great War, and the Remaking of America*. Baltimore: Johns Hopkins University Press, 2001.

Kennedy, David M. *Over Here: The First World War and American Society*. Oxford: Oxford University Press, 1980.

Kleber, Brooks E., and Dale Birdsell. *The Chemical Warfare Service: Chemicals in Combat*. Washington: U.S. GPO, 2003.

Kreidberg, Marvin A., and Merton G. Henry. *History of Military Mobilization in the United States Army: 1775–1945*. Washington: U.S. GPO, 1955.

Lamb, Arthur B., Robert E. Wilson, and N. K. Chaney. "Gas Mask Absorbents." *Journal of Industrial and Engineering Chemistry* 11, no. 5 (May 1919): 420–38.

Langer, William L., and Robert B. MacMullin. *With "E" of the First Gas*. New York: Holton, 1919.

Laurie, Clayton D., and Ronald H. Cole. *The Role of Federal Military Forces in Domestic Disorders: 1877–1945*. Washington: U.S. GPO, 1997.

Lemons, J. Stanley. *The Woman Citizen: Social Feminism in the 1920s*. Charlottesville: University Press of Virginia, 1990.

Lengel, Edward G. *To Conquer Hell: The Meuse-Argonne, 1918*. New York: Holt, 2008.

"Lenroot Impressed at Edgewood." *Chemical and Metallurgical Engineering* 24, no. 15 (April 13, 1921): 668.

Link, Arthur Stanley. *The Impact of World War I*. New York: Harper and Row, 1969.

Loach, William B. "Mustard Gas Production in the United States." *Chemical Warfare* 1, no. 10 (October 23, 1919): 8–14.

"Major-General Gilchrist Heads C.W.S." *Chemical and Metallurgical Engineering* 36, no. 4 (April 1929): 259.

"Major-General Sibert and 'New York Times' Discuss Gas Warfare." *Chemical Warfare* 1, no. 9 (October 16, 1919): 2–3.

March, Peyton C. *The Nation at War*. New York: Doubleday, Doran, 1932.

Mauroni, Albert J. *America's Struggle with Chemical-Biological Warfare*. Westport, Conn.: Praeger, 2000.

———. *Chemical Demilitarization: Public Policy Aspects*. Westport, Conn.: Praeger, 2003.

———. "The U.S. Army Chemical Corps: Past, Present, and Future." *On Point: The Journal of Army History* 9, no. 3 (Winter 2004): 9–14.

Mead, Gary. *The Doughboys: America and the First World War*. Woodstock: Overlook, 2000.

Miller, Edward S. *War Plan Orange: The U.S. Strategy to Defeat Japan, 1897–1945*. Annapolis: Naval Institute Press, 1991.

Millett, Allan R., and Peter Maslowski. *For the Common Defense: A Military History of the United States of America*. New York: Free Press, 1984.

Murphy, Paul L. *The Meaning of the Freedom of Speech: First Amendment Freedoms from Wilson to FDR*. Westport, Conn.: Greenwood, 1972.

Murray, Williamson, and Allan R. Millett. *Military Innovation in the Interwar Period*. Cambridge: Cambridge University Press, 1996.

The National in the World War: April 6, 1917–November 11, 1918. Cleveland: General Electric, 1920.

"Naval Influence in Abolishing Chemical Warfare." *Chemical and Metallurgical Engineering* 26, no. 2 (January 18, 1922): 1.

Ndiaye, Pap A. *Nylon and Bombs: DuPont and the March of Modern America.* Baltimore, Md.: Johns Hopkins University Press, 2007.

Nielsen, Kim E. *Un-American Womanhood: Antiradicalism, Antifeminism, and the First Red Scare.* Columbus: Ohio State Press, 2001.

Odom, William O. *After the Trenches: The Transformation of U.S. Army Doctrine, 1918–1939.* College Station: Texas A&M University Press, 1999.

Palazzo, Albert. *Seeking Victory on the Western Front: The British Army and Chemical Warfare in World War I.* Lincoln: University of Nebraska, 2000.

Parsons, Charles L. "The American Chemist in Warfare." *Journal of Industrial and Engineering Chemistry* 10, no. 10 (October 1918): 776.

Pershing, John J. *Final Report of John J. Pershing: Commander-in-Chief American Expeditionary Forces.* Washington: U.S. GPO, 1919.

"Philadelphia Meeting, American Chemical Society." *Chemical and Metallurgical Engineering* 21, no. 6 (September 15, 1919): 279.

Prentiss, Augustin M. *Chemicals in War: A Treatise on Chemical Warfare.* New York: McGraw-Hill, 1937.

"The Present Status of American Chemists and War Service." *Journal of Industrial and Engineering Chemistry* 9, no. 7 (July 1, 1917): 639.

"Present Strength of the Chemical Warfare Service." *Chemical and Metallurgical Engineering* 21, no. 12 (November 12–19, 1919): 610.

Price, Richard M. *The Chemical Weapons Taboo.* Ithaca, N.Y.: Cornell University Press, 1997.

Pultz, David. *A Preaching Ministry: Twenty-One Sermons Preached by Harry Emerson Fosdick at the First Presbyterian Church in the City of New York, 1918–1925.* New York: First Presbyterian Church in the City of New York, 2000.

"Readers 'Tenshun.'" *Chemical Warfare* 1, no. 1 (August 21, 1919).

Reed, Germaine M. *Crusading for Chemistry: The Professional Career of Charles Holmes Herty.* Athens: The University of Georgia Press, 1995.

Richter, Donald. *Chemical Soldiers: British Gas Warfare in World War I.* Lawrence: University Press of Kansas, 1992.

Rosenman, Samuel I., ed., Donald. *The Public Papers and Addresses of Franklin D. Roosevelt: 1943 Volume, The Tide Turns.* New York: Harper, 1950.

Ross, Steven T. *American War Plans: 1919–1941.* 5 vols. New York: Garland, 1992.

———. *American War Plans: 1890–1939.* London: Cass, 2002.

Russell, Edmund. *War and Nature: Fighting Humans and Insects with Chemicals from World War I to Silent Spring.* Cambridge: Cambridge University Press, 2001.

Scharf, Louis, and Joan M. Jensen. *Decades of Discontent: The Women's Movement, 1920–1940.* Boston: Northeastern University Press, 1987.

"Scrapping War Chemicals." *Chemical and Metallurgical Engineering* 20, no. 3 (February 1, 1919): 97–98.

Slotten, Hugh R. "Humane Chemistry or Scientific Barbarism? American Responses to World War I Poison Gas, 1915–1930." *Journal of American History* 77, no. 2 (September 1990): 476–98.

Smith, Gene. *Until the Last Trumpet Sounds: The Life of General of the Armies John J. Pershing.* New York: Wiley, 1998.

Smythe, Donald. *Pershing, General of the Armies.* Bloomington: Indiana University Press, 2007.

Bibliography

Spiers, Edward M. *Chemical and Biological Weapons: A Study in Proliferation.* New York: St. Martin's, 1994.

Statistical Abstracts of the United States. No. 44 (1921). Washington: U.S. GPO, 1922.

Stockholm International Peace Research Institute. *The Problem of Chemical and Biological Warfare: A Study of the Historical, Technical, Military, Legal, and Political Aspects of CBW, and Possible Disarmament Measures.* 6 vols. Stockholm: Almqvist & Wiksell, 1971–1975.

"Transfer of the Experiment Station at American University to the War Department." *Journal of Industrial and Engineering Chemistry* 10, no. 8 (August 1918): 654.

Tuorinsky, Shirley D. *Medical Aspects of Chemical Warfare.* Washington: Office of the Surgeon General, 2008.

"United States Chemical Warfare Service—II." *Scientific American* 120, no. 15 (April 12, 1919): 372–3.

"Universal Gas Mask." *Chemical and Metallurgical Engineering* 28, no. 22 (June 4, 1923): 982.

"U.S. Army Reserve of Gas Material." *Chemical Warfare* 1, no. 9 (October 16, 1919): 12.

U.S. House of Representatives Select Committee on Expenditures in the War Department. *War Expenditures: Hearings before Subcommittee No. 3 (Foreign Expenditures) of the Select Committee on Expenditures in the War Department, House of Representatives, 66th Congress, 2nd Session, on War Expenditures, Volume 2.* Washington: U.S. GPO, 1920.

U.S. House of Representatives and U.S. Senate Committees on Military Affairs. *Army Reorganization, Gen. John J. Pershing: Joint Hearings Before the Committees on Military Affairs, House of Representatives and United States Senate, 66th Congress, 1st Session, on H.R. 8287, H.R. 8068, H.R. 7925, H.R. 8870, Part 29.* Washington: U.S. GPO, 1919.

U.S. Senate Committee on the Judiciary. *Alleged Dye Monopoly: Hearings before a Subcommittee of the Committee on the Judiciary, United States Senate, 67th Congress, 2nd Session.* Washington: U.S. GPO, 1922.

U.S. Senate Committee on Military Affairs. *Reorganization of the Army: Hearings on S. 2691, S. 2693, and S. 2715, 66th Congress, 1st Session.* Washington: U.S. GPO, 1922.

U.S. Surgeon General's Office. *The Medical Department of the United States Army in the World War: Volume XIV, Medical Aspects of Gas Warfare.* Washington: U.S. GPO, 1926.

———. *The Medical Department of the United States Army in the World War: Volume XV, Statistics, Part Two.* Washington: U.S. GPO, 1925.

U.S. War Department. *Report of the Secretary of War to the President: 1922.* Washington: U.S. GPO, 1922.

Vandiver, Frank E. *Black Jack: the Life and Times of John J. Pershing.* College Station: Texas A&M University Press, 1977.

Vedder, Edward B., and Harold P. Sawyer. "Chlorine as a Therapeutic Agent in Certain Respiratory Diseases." *Journal of the American Medical Association.* 82, no. 10 (March 8, 1924): 764–6.

———. "The Present Status of Chlorine Gas Therapy." *Annuals of Clinical Medicine* 4 (1925): 21–9.
———. *The Medical Aspects of Chemical Warfare*. Baltimore: Williams and Wilkins, 1925.
Vilensky, Joel A. *Dew of Death: The Story of Lewisite, America's World War I Weapon of Mass Destruction*. Bloomington: Indiana University Press, 2005.
Vilensky, Joel A., and Pandy R. Sinish. "Blisters as Weapons of War: The Vesicants of World War I." *Chemical Heritage* 24, no. 2 (Summer 2006): 12–17.
Waitt, Alden H. *Gas Warfare: The Chemical Weapon, Its Use, and Protection against It*. New York: Duell, Sloan, and Pearce, 1943.
Waller, Douglas. *A Question of Loyalty: Gen. Billy Mitchell and the Court-Martial That Gripped the Nation*. New York: Harper Collins, 2004.
"War Department Deserts Chemical Warfare Service." *Chemical and Metallurgical Engineering* 21, no. 4 (August 15, 1919): 165.
"[The] War Department Discovers the Chemist." *Chemical and Metallurgical Engineering* 18, no. 4 (February 15, 1918): 165.
"Warning! Beware the Gas-Mask!" *Chemical and Metallurgical Engineering* 20, no. 7 (April 1, 1919): 305–6.
"War on Rats with Poison Gas." *Chemical and Metallurgical Engineering* 23, no. 11 (September 15, 1920): 543.
"War Service of Chemists." *Journal of Industrial and Engineering Chemistry* 9, no. 8 (August 1917): 730.
Whittemore, Gilbert F. "World War I, Poison Gas Research, and the Ideals of American Chemists." *Social Studies of Science* 5, no. 2 (May 1975): 135–63.
Yerkes, Robert M. *The New World of Science: Its Development During the War*. New York: Century, 1920.

INDEX

1st Gas Regiment, 49, 50–53, 61
30th Engineers, 35–37, 48–49

Addison, James Thayer, 37, 49, 51
airplanes: and chemical weapons, 54, 58, 83, 93–95; and protective devices, 110–11; and smoke, 111
Air Service, 61, 93–95
American Chemical Society, 15, 41, 69–70
American University, 14, 19, 72, 73
animal traps, 96
Ansauville, 31
artillery: casualties, 31, 34; and chemical warfare, 11, 25, 37–39, 53; coastal, 94, 110; French, 36, 37, 48; German, 1, 31, 36, 48, 49, 52; German shells, 9; at Lahayville, 48; at Saint-Mihiel, 50; shell manufacturing, 20, 21, 39, 44, 47, 93; and protective devices, 28, 39; wounds compared with gas, 57, 65, 73
Atkisson, Earl J., 4, 61, 92–93, 104–5
Auld, Samuel J. M., 20

Baccarat, 49
Baker, Newton D., 13, 41–43, 72, 74
Battery De Russey, 110
Black, William M., 24–25, 61
Bliss, Tasker H., 16
Bogert, Marston T., 41, 44
Bois de Remieres, 31–32
Bolimov, 9
Borah, William E., 107–9
British: censorship before 1917, 12–13; and chemical warfare before 1917, 9–12; comparisons with U.S., 3, 14, 32, 47, 57; research collaborations with U.S., 16–19, 66; supplying the U.S., 3, 23, 27, 29, 39, 47, 54; training U.S. personnel, 3, 20, 23, 35, 38. *See also* Small Box Respirator
Bureau of Mines: gas mask work, 15–17, 28–29, 80; initiates chemical warfare research, 3, 13–15; July 1917 reorganization, 19–20; June 1918 reorganization, 39–43; mustard gas research, 17–19
Burrell, George A., 13, 15, 41, 43
Burton, Theodore E., 103–5, 107, 108

casualties, chemical warfare: causes of, 31–32, 34–35, 48, 49–50; first U.S., 31; persistency of symptoms, 67, 90–92; statistics about, 11, 32, 57, 65–67, 125n51; treatment of, 18–19, 32–33
Chamberlain, George E., 61–62, 71, 75
Chateau-Thierry, 36–37
Chaumont, 23
chemical manufacturers: Chemical Warfare Service work, 4–5, 62–63, 68–69; ethics, 92; and protectionism, 68, 85, 89–90, 108
Chemical Service Section: 30th Engineers, 35; and artillery, 37–38; becomes Chemical Warfare Service, 3, 39–42; and defensive equipment, 27, 29–30; gas officers, 31, 34, 35; training 22–27, 32
chemical warfare: as barbaric, 3–4, 10, 57–58, 114, 115–16; as humane, 65–66, 73, 91, 98, 115–16.

145

chemical warfare (*continued*): See also Geneva Gas Protocol (1925); Hague Peace Declaration (1899); Washington Conference on the Limitation of Armaments (1921–1922)

Chemical Warfare (journal), 63–65

chemical weapons: attacks, January-May 1918, 1–2, 30–32, 33–34; attacks, June-November 1918, 49, 51–52; effectiveness, 36, 55, 66–67; effects of weather, 2, 10, 38–39, 48; effects on morale, 2, 11, 25–26, 38; first uses, 8–10; used by AEF, 35–36, 48–49, 50, 52–53; used by AEF artillery, 37–39, 48

chlorine: manufacturing, 44–45, 47; as medicine, 97–99; storage and transportation, 67, 73; use, 7, 9–10, 11, 24–25

civil disorder, 99–101

Civil War, U.S., 7–8

Color Plans: defined, 85; Plan Green, 85–88; Plan Yellow, 111

Conant, James B., 19, 45, 54

Congress, U.S.: and Geneva Gas Protocol (1925), 107–10, 115; lobbied by Chemical Warfare Service, 4, 56, 62–63, 70, 89; and National Defense Act (1919), 61–62; and National Defense Act (1920), 68, 71–75; and tariffs, 68, 89–90

Coolidge, Calvin, 98, 104, 107

Corps of Engineers: and chemical service section, 3, 22, 35; chemical warfare responsibilities, 20, 24–25, 42; postwar reassignment of chemical warfare personnel, 61; proposed absorption of Chemical Warfare Service, 59, 71–72

Cox, James M., 57

Crowell, Benedict, 12, 16–17, 41

cylinders, gas, 9, 10, 11, 24–25

Davis, Dwight F., 112–13

Department of State, 3, 83–84, 104–5, 107

Dewey, Bradley, 14, 16

disease, poison gas as cure for, 5, 97–99, 108

Dorsey, Frank M., 45, 54, 74

Doughty, John W., 7

Drum, Hugh A., 80–81

Dulles, Allen Welsh, 105

dye industry, 4, 68, 85, 89–90

Edgewood Arsenal: after armistice, 67–68, 70, 78, 81, 100; and Amos A. Fries, 60, 63–64, 73, 74, 81; and chlorine gas "cure," 97–98; demonstrations at, 80, 89, 94, 97, 100; in 1918, 44–48, 53; initial construction, 20–21; and William H. Walker, 44, 59, 74

Edison, Thomas A., 96

Eisenhower, Dwight D., 113

Fish, Hamilton, III, 109

Forbes, Charles R., 91

Fort Monroe, 110

Fosdick, Harry Emerson, 58

Foulkes, Charles H., 11, 23

French: blamed for casualties, 34–35; censorship before 1917, 12–13; chemical warfare before 1917, 8–12; chemical warfare operations with U.S., 3, 30, 36, 48–49, 51; comparisons with U.S., 32, 37, 47; supplying and training U.S., 38, 47. See also Tissot mask

French, John, 10

Frelinghuysen, Joseph H., 74

Fries, Amos A.: airplanes, 54, 93–94, 95; biographical information, 59–60; British equipment, 23, 54; Chemical Warfare Service independence, 59; communism, 102–3; dyes, 90; Edgewood Arsenal, 47–48, 67, 70–71; family, 73, 74, 100, 103; gas mask reserve, 80–83, 111–12, 113; John Thomas Taylor, 108; medical effects of gas exposure, 91, 98–99; mustard gas, 18, 47; National Defense Act (1919), 61–62; opinions about chemical warfare, 2, 5, 65–67, 84, 115; postwar transfers, 61; promotion to chief, 75–76; public relations work, 4, 62–65, 71, 89; reorganization hearings, 72–75;

research, 18, 89; retirement, 5, 113; safe security devices, 97; structure of chemical warfare forces, 78–79; tear gas, 99–100; war plans, 85–87; Washington Conference on the Limitation of Armaments (1921–1922), 83–84; writings, 65, 96, 102
Fries, Elizabeth (daughter), 100
Fries, Elizabeth (Mrs. Amos A. Fries), 103

gas. *See* chemical weapons
gas baseball, 23
gas chamber, 101–2
gas masks: abandoned after armistice, 61; for airplanes, 95, 110–11; development, 10–11, 28–29, 80; manufacture, 16–17, 111–12; marketed after armistice, 79–80; research, 13, 14, 15–16; reserve, 80–83, 112–13; training, 23–26. *See also* Small Box Respirator; Tissot mask
gas officers: reports, 2, 34–35, 50, 52; responsibilities, 26, 34, 48; training observations, 24, 25
Gee Jon, 101
General Electric, 14, 15
Geneva Gas Protocol (1925): negotiation, 103–6; ratification, 106–10, 115
Germans: and chemical warfare before 1917, 2, 8–11, 57; chemical weapons destroyed after armistice, 60–61; comparisons with U.S., 14, 32, 47, 57, 66; dye industry, 68, 85; mustard gas, 17, 19, 47; U.S. fear of retaliation, 26, 36, 39, 50–51, 114; and World War II, 113–14. *See also* chemical weapons
Gilchrist, Harry L., 29, 32–33, 134n33
Goodrich Rubber Company, 16, 17
Gorgas, William C., 13
Grant, Ulysses S., 8

Haber, Fritz, 9, 57
Hague Peace Declaration (1899), 2, 8, 9, 10
Haldane, John Burdon Sanderson, 57
Hale, George Ellery, 92
Hall, Robert A., 35

Hanlon, Joseph T., 48
Hanlon (Experimental) Field, 23, 48
Hanson, H. H., 45, 46
Hawaii, 77–78, 82, 112
Heflin, James Thomas, 109
Herty, Charles H.: and Bureau of Mines, 43; and Chemical Warfare Service, 69–70, 73–74, 75; and Washington Conference on the Limitation of Armaments (1921–1922), 85
Hughes, Charles Evans, 83

Irwin, Will, 58

Kahn, Julius, 61–62, 71
Kellogg, Frank B., 107
King, William Henry, 90

La Ferme Saint Marie, 35–36
Lahayville, 48
Lane, Franklin K., 13, 40–41
Lewis, Winford Lee, 54
Lewisite, 54–55, 111
Livens projectors: compared to artillery, 37, 53; first use against the AEF, 31–32; introduction, 12; supplied by the British, 23; used by the U.S., 36, 49, 52, 53–54
Loach, William B., 46
Loos, 10

Manning, Van H.: Gas Investigations Division work 13–15, 16; opposes consolidation, 41–43
March, Peyton C.: and consolidation of Chemical Warfare Service, 41, 42; and overseas garrisons, 77–78; postwar opposition to Chemical Warfare Service, 58, 61, 71–73, 74
Maxwell, Lucia R., 102–3
McCullough, Ernest, 37–38
Medical Department. *See* Surgeon General's Office
Meuse-Argonne, 50, 51–52
Mexico, 85–88
military industrial complex, 5, 113
Mitchell, William "Billy," 93, 94–95
mobilization plans, 78–79

mortars: and chemical warfare, 11, 23, 37, 49, 52; high-explosive, 31, 48

mustard gas: attacks, July 1917-May 1918, 1, 17, 31, 34; attacks, June-November 1918, 35, 49–50, 52; manufacture, 19, 45–47; properties, 17–19, 32–33, 37; protective devices, 28–29, 111; safe security devices, 96

National Defense Act (1919), 61–62, 68

National Defense Act (1920): and chemists, 68, 69, 70; as foundation for CWS's public relations work, 4, 77, 103; hearings, 71–76; and John J. Pershing, 58–59

National Defense Test Day (1924), 80–82

Nernst, Walther, 9

Neuve-Chapelle, 9

Nichols, William H., 41

Nieuwland, Julius Arthur, 54

Nixon, Richard M., 115

Ordnance Department: and chemical warfare organization, 3, 20, 42, 59, 92–93; and Edgewood Arsenal, 20–21, 44

Overman Act, 42

overseas territories. *See* Hawaii; Panama; Philippines

Panama: Chemical Warfare Service garrison, 77–78; gas mask reserve, 82, 112; postwar chlorine reserve, 67; shore batteries, 110

Parsons, Charles L., 15

Pershing, John J.: opinions on chemical weapons, 54, 58–59, 109; and overseas garrisons, 78; support for consolidation, 42; and William L. Sibert, 40

pesticides, 4, 95–96, 111, 113

Philippines, The: 1927 war exercise, 111; Amos A. Fries in, 59, 61; Chemical Warfare Service garrison, 77–78, 105; gas mask reserve, 82, 112; shore batteries, 110

phosgene: first use, 10–11; at Lahayville, 48; manufacture, 44; postwar reserve, 67; used against AEF, 31, 34, 52; used by AEF, 36, 37

poison gas. *See* chemical weapons

Pope, William, 19

Popenoe, Wilson, 88

Porter, William N., 80, 114

protection devices, 29–30, 110–11. *See also* gas masks

Rambervillers, 48–49

research laboratories: American University, 14, 19, 72, 73; Catholic University, 14, 54; General Electric, 14, 15; Harvard University, 14, 19; Johns Hopkins University, 14, 69; MIT, 14, 15; Willoughby, 54–55

Roosevelt, Franklin D., 114

Russians, 8, 9, 10, 82

safe security devices, 96–97

Saint Mihiel, 34, 35, 36, 50–51

Scott, Nathan Bay, 72, 73, 126–27n72

Seicheprey, 49

shell-filling, 21, 44

Shepherd, Forest, 7–8

Sibert, William L.: appointed to Chemical Service Section, 39–40; at army reorganization hearings, 72–73, 74; chemical warfare "not a fad," 55; consolidation of chemical warfare, 40–42; and dye industry, 90; leader of postwar CWS, 60; and Mexico, 86; retirement, 75–76

Small Box Respirator: discomfort, 27–28; misuse, 1, 28, 49; Tissot used instead of, 28, 35, 39; U.S. versions, 16–17, 28–29. *See also* gas masks

smoke: research, 19, 53, 94, 111; use during World War I, 11, 36, 37, 50, 52, 53

spider web chart, 102–3, 132n127

St. Petersburg Declaration (1868), 8

Surgeon General's Office: casualty

statistics, 57, 65–66, 125n51; and chemical warfare organization, 3, 40, 42; chemical warfare training, 20, 22; gas mask development, 13, 16–17, 19, 20. *See also* casualties

tariffs, 4, 68, 89–90
tear gas: airplane bombs, 94, 95, 99–100; in law enforcement, 99–101, 102; manufacture, 44; potential use in Mexico, 86, 88; use during World War I, 1, 8–9, 11, 17, 31
thermite, 54
Tissot mask, 28–29, 35, 39
training, 3, 20, 22–26

Vedder, Edward B., 91, 98

Veterans' Bureau, 91, 108
Vogelsang, Alexander, 41–42

Wadsworth, James W. Jr., 69, 107–8
Walker, William H., 44, 59, 74
Washington Conference on the Limitation of Armaments (1921–1922), 59, 83–85, 104
Weeks, John W., 77, 81, 82, 98
West, Clarence J., 2, 96
Wilson, Woodrow, 40–41, 42–43
Wood, Leonard, 99
World War II, 96, 113–14

Ypres: first chlorine attack, 8, 9–10, 12; mustard gas, 17, 18, 19; phosgene, 10–11

THOMAS I. FAITH is a historian at the U.S. Department of State.

The University of Illinois Press
is a founding member of the
Association of American University Presses.

___

Composed in 9.5/12.5 Trump Mediaeval
by Lisa Connery
at the University of Illinois Press
Manufactured by Cushing-Malloy, Inc.

University of Illinois Press
1325 South Oak Street
Champaign, IL 61820-6903
www.press.uillinois.edu